McGraw-Hill Education
REASONING THROUGH LANGUAGE ARTS (RLA)
WORKBOOK
FOR THE
GED® TEST

SECOND EDITION

McGraw-Hill Education

REASONING THROUGH LANGUAGE ARTS (RLA)

WORKBOOK

FOR THE

GED® TEST

SECOND EDITION

McGraw-Hill Education Editors

Contributor: Jouve North America

New York Chicago San Francisco Athens London Madrid
Mexico City Milan New Delhi Singapore Sydney Toronto

Copyright © 2019, by McGraw-Hill Education LLC. All rights reserved. Except as permitted under the United States Copyright Act of 1976, no part of this publication may be reproduced or distributed in any form or by any means, or stored in a database or retrieval system, without the prior written permission of the publisher.

1 2 3 4 5 6 7 8 9   LHS   23 22 21 20 19 18

ISBN: 978-1-260-12070-7
MHID: 1-260-12070-8

e-ISBN: 978-1-260-12071-4
e-MHID: 1-260-12071-6

GED® is a registered trademark of the American Council on Education (ACE) and administered exclusively by GED Testing Service LLC under license. This content is not endorsed or approved by ACE or GED Testing Service.

McGraw-Hill Education products are available at special quantity discounts to use as premiums and sales promotions or for use in corporate training programs. To contact a representative, please visit the Contact Us pages at www.mhprofessional.com.

Contents

Introduction — vii
How to Use This Workbook — vii
The GED® Reasoning through Language Arts Test — viii
The Top 25 Things You Need to Know for the GED® RLA Test — x

REASONING THROUGH LANGUAGE ARTS PRETEST — 1

Answers and Explanations — 30
Evaluation Chart — 34

CHAPTER 1 Grammar and Conventions — 35

CHAPTER 2 Informational Texts — 51

CHAPTER 3 Argumentation and Persuasion — 67

CHAPTER 4 Literature — 85

CHAPTER 5 Extended Response — 111

Answers and Explanations — 117

REASONING THROUGH LANGUAGE ARTS POSTTEST — 127

Answers and Explanations — 160
Evaluation Chart — 163

Introduction

How to Use This Workbook

This workbook contains practice problems to help you sharpen your skills in preparation for taking the GED® Reasoning through Language Arts (RLA) test.

Start your RLA practice by taking the **Reasoning through Language Arts Pretest** at the beginning of this workbook. It will help you decide which chapters of the workbook will be most valuable to you. You will also see some samples of the special question formats that appear on the actual exam.

Take the Pretest in a controlled environment, with as few distractions as possible. If you want to more closely simulate testing conditions, limit yourself to 150 minutes, although you may prefer taking the test untimed in order to get a chance to read each passage carefully and to think about each question.

When you are done, or when time is up, check your answers in the Answers and Explanations, where you will find short explanations of the correct response to each question. Next, find the problem numbers you answered incorrectly in the Evaluation Chart to identify the chapters on which you need to concentrate.

The book is divided into four sections, each devoted to a specific type of text you will encounter on the RLA. There are several different passages, or text samples, to give you an idea of the texts that will appear on the test and types of questions you may be asked. The questions have also been carefully designed to match each of the following:

- the test content
- the "depth of knowledge" (DOK) levels that measure how well you understand each topic
- the Common Core State Standards (CCSS) that you are expected to have mastered

Answers are located at the back of the workbook.

Finally, when you have completed the last exercise, take the **Reasoning through Language Arts Posttest** at the back of this book. This test can help you reevaluate yourself after practicing as much of the workbook as you feel is necessary. It also contains more samples of the special question formats used on the real exam. Answers are located at the end of the test, and another Evaluation Chart is provided to help you decide if you are ready to take the GED® Reasoning through Language Arts test or where you might need further practice.

The GED® Reasoning through Language Arts Test

The GED® Reasoning through Language Arts Test is a computer-based test, which allows for a broad range of item types. Most questions on the test will be multiple-choice items, each of which has four answer choices from which to choose. You will also encounter a smaller number of technology-based items. These come in a variety of formats such as fill-in-the-blank, drop-down, and drag-and-drop.

- **Fill-in-the-blank:** These are short-answer items in which a response may be entered directly from the keyboard.

- **Drop-down:** A list of possible responses is displayed when the response area is clicked with the mouse.

- **Drag-and-drop:** Words are "dragged" around the screen by pointing at them with the mouse, holding the mouse button down, and then releasing the button when the word is positioned over an area on the screen.

Seventy-five percent of the texts on which the questions are based are informational texts on a variety of topics. These texts are based on real-world situations and experiences. They fall into three categories:

- Workplace documents or other documents you might find in your everyday life, such as memoranda, brochures, instructions, handbooks, flyers, and business letters.

- Science documents that generally focus on human health and living systems (nutrition, physical fitness) and energy (conservation, energy production, etc.).

- Social studies documents that focus on American civics, including documents based in American government, such as presidential speeches, and other primary or secondary American historical documents.

Twenty-five percent of the texts will test your knowledge of literature; however, the test focuses solely on fiction, such as short stories, and does not include poetry or drama.

Twenty percent of the overall number of questions will test your ability to edit sentences in workplace or other everyday documents so they are grammatically correct and follow the conventions of standard American English.

You will also be asked to produce a writing sample, also called an Extended Response. You will have 45 minutes to write a response to a prompt. The prompt will require you to analyze one or more brief source texts, then support your analysis with evidence from the source texts. These texts may focus on two sides of a specific issue, which each writer supports with some kind of evidence.

You will be scored using a scoring rubric on three traits:

- Analyzing an argument using evidence
- Developing and organizing your ideas
- Clarity of the writing and correct use of the conventions of standard American English

If you are taking the GED on computer, you will need to type your essay, so you may need to brush up on your typing skills. Visit http://www.ged.com for more about the GED® Test.

The Top 25 Things You Need to Know for the GED® RLA Test

Use this list as a guide for your studies. Be sure to study and practice each topic until you feel that you have mastered it.

1. **Main Idea:** Know how to identify the main idea of a paragraph or passage.
2. **Structural Relationships:** Identify cause-and-effect, compare-and-contrast, and parallel relationships. Be able to identify sequence of events.
3. **Vocabulary:** Know how to find context clues and know the difference between connotation and denotation; identify synonyms and antonyms for words.
4. **Figurative Language:** Understand simile, metaphor, and personification.
5. **Author's Views:** Identify an author's tone, point of view, and purpose.
6. **Rhetorical Techniques:** Know the ways in which writers use language to convey meaning through analogy, enumeration, juxtaposition, parallelism, qualifying statement, and repetition.
7. **Evidence:** Identify supporting evidence (facts, statistics, expert opinions, and anecdotes), and evaluate evidence for relevancy, reliability, reasonableness, and sufficiency.
8. **Opinion and Bias:** Know the difference between fact and opinion; identify bias.
9. **Logical Fallacies:** Identify errors in the logical reasoning of an author's argument.
10. **Argument Structure:** Be able to identify the conclusion and supporting evidence of an argument.
11. **Analyzing Data:** Know how to read charts and graphs and draw conclusions from them.
12. **Perspective:** Understand the difference between the point of view of the narrator and that of characters.
13. **Inference:** Draw conclusions from information given in a text.
14. **Parts of Speech:** Know these parts of speech and their functions: noun, pronoun, verb, adjective, adverb, preposition, conjunction.
15. **Subject–Verb Agreement:** Know how to construct sentences in which the subject and verb agree; know how to fix a sentence in which the subject and verb do not agree.

16. **Pronoun Agreement:** Know how to construct sentences in which the pronouns agree with their antecedents; know how to fix a mistake in pronoun agreement.

17. **Pronoun Case:** Understand the subjective, objective, and possessive cases for pronouns; use the correct case for pronouns; fix mistakes in pronoun case.

18. **Modifiers:** Understand how modifiers are used, and correct modifiers that are misplaced or dangling.

19. **Capitalization:** Know the rules of capitalization and correct capitalization errors.

20. **Sentence Construction:** Recognize and correct sentence fragments and run-on sentences.

21. **Comma Usage:** Know when a comma should be used and how to correct comma errors.

22. **Other Punctuation:** Know the proper use of apostrophes, colons, and semicolons; know how to use end marks and abbreviations; correct punctuation errors.

23. **Verb Tenses:** Know how to form simple, present perfect, and past perfect tenses, and correct errors in verb tense.

24. **Parallel Structure:** Create parallel structure in a sentence; recognize an error in parallelism; correct an error in parallelism.

25. **Essay Structure:** Know the proper structure to use for an effective essay response.

PRETEST
Reasoning through Language Arts

This Pretest is intended to give you an idea of the topics you need to study to pass the GED® Reasoning through Language Arts Test. Try to work on the Pretest in a quiet area so you are free from distractions, and give yourself enough time. The time allotted for the Pretest is 150 minutes, but it is more important to be sure you get a chance to think about every question than it is to finish ahead of time. The GED® Reasoning through Language Arts Test also includes a written response section, known as the Extended Response. See Chapter 5 for two examples of that component of the test.

Answers and explanations for every question can be found at the end of the Pretest.

Part 1: 22 questions | **35 minutes**

The following memo contains several numbered blanks, each marked "`Select... ▼`*". Beneath each one is a set of choices. Indicate the choice from each set that is correct and belongs in the blank. (**Note:** On the real GED® test, the choices will appear as a "drop-down" menu. When you click on a choice, it will appear in the blank.)*

Special Announcement to all Employees

Great news! In response to all your requests, the company is planning to open a child-care facility on the third floor.

The target opening is set for May 15. All those who want to register a child must stop by HR and pick up the necessary forms. Have your `1. Select... ▼` sign the forms. The completed forms must be returned to HR before a child can attend. You also need to fill out an information form so there will be a record of any emergency numbers that may be needed.

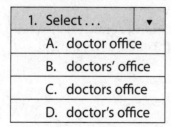

Unfortunately, there is a limit on the number of children who can be cared for at the facility, `2. Select... ▼` sooner rather than later. But we will be creating a wait list, should more parents apply than we can handle.

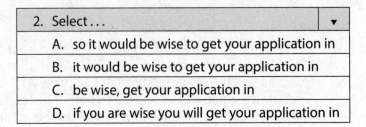

2. Select...
A.	so it would be wise to get your application in
B.	it would be wise to get your application in
C.	be wise, get your application in
D.	if you are wise you will get your application in

A hot lunch will be provided by the new facility, made possible because of the large kitchen area on the third floor. If your child has special dietary needs, you will have to make that clear on the application and 3. Select... . Snacks will also be provided, but if a parent prefers, 4. Select... .

3. Select...
A.	provides a list of foods that is acceptable
B.	provide a list of foods that is acceptable
C.	provides a list of foods that are acceptable
D.	provide a list of foods that are acceptable

4. Select...
A.	a child may bring their own food
B.	a child may bring his or her own food
C.	a child may bring his or hers own food
D.	a child may bring its own food

The facility will be open Monday through Friday, 7:30 a.m. to 5:30 p.m. 5. Select... . She will have five assistants. We are seeking an adult to child ratio of one to ten. The cost will vary depending on your current salary; 6. Select... . The company sees no need to make a profit from the day care; all that is needed is to cover costs of personnel and food as well other expenses.

If you have any questions, contact Ben Westin in Human Resources. We are all very excited by this new development.

5. Select... ▼
A. With 22 years of child-care experience, it will be under the supervision of Celeste Lane.
B. Celeste Lane who has 22 years of child-care supervision, it will be under her supervision.
C. It will be under the supervision of Celeste Lane, who has 22 years of child-care experience.
D. Under the supervision of Celeste Lane it will be, with 22 years of child-care experience.

6. Select... ▼
A. however, we want to make the facility affordable for you.
B. in addition, we want to make the facility affordable for you.
C. consequently, we want to make the facility affordable for you.
D. otherwise, we want to make the facility affordable for you.

Use the pair of passages to answer Questions 7–17.

Adapted from a speech by President Franklin Roosevelt (1941)

1   Just as our national policy in internal affairs has been based upon a decent respect for the rights and the dignity of all our fellow men within our gates, so our national policy in foreign affairs has been based on a decent respect for the rights and the dignity of all nations, large and small. And the justice of morality must and will win in the end.

2   Our national policy is this:

3   First, by an impressive expression of the public will and without regard to partisanship, we are committed to all-inclusive national defense.

4   Second, by an impressive expression of the public will and without regard to partisanship, we are committed to full support of all those resolute people everywhere who are resisting aggression and are thereby keeping war away from our hemisphere. By this support we express our determination that the democratic cause shall prevail, and we strengthen the defense and the security of our own nation.

5   Third, by an impressive expression of the public will and without regard to partisanship, we are committed to the proposition that principles of morality and considerations for our own security will never permit us to acquiesce in a peace dictated by aggressors and sponsored by appeasers. We

know that enduring peace cannot be bought at the cost of other people's freedom.

6. In the recent national election there was no substantial difference between the two great parties in respect to that national policy. No issue was fought out on this line before the American electorate. And today it is abundantly evident that American citizens everywhere are demanding and supporting speedy and complete action in recognition of obvious danger.

7. Therefore, the immediate need is a swift and driving increase in our armament production. Leaders of industry and labor have responded to our summons. Goals of speed have been set. In some cases these goals are being reached ahead of time. In some cases we are on schedule; in other cases there are slight but not serious delays. And in some cases—and, I am sorry to say, very important cases—we are all concerned by the slowness of the accomplishment of our plans....

8. No matter whether the original goal was set too high or too low, our objective is quicker and better results.

9. To give you two illustrations:

10. We are behind schedule in turning out finished airplanes. We are working day and night to solve the innumerable problems and to catch up.

11. We are ahead of schedule in building warships, but we are working to get even further ahead of that schedule.

12. To change a whole nation from a basis of peacetime production of implements of peace to a basis of wartime production of implements of war is no small task. And the greatest difficulty comes at the beginning of the program, when new tools, new plant facilities, new assembly lines, new shipways must first be constructed before the actual material begins to flow steadily and speedily from them....

13. New circumstances are constantly begetting new needs for our safety. I shall ask this Congress for greatly increased new appropriations and authorizations to carry on what we have begun.

Excerpt from the Farewell Address by President Dwight Eisenhower (1961)

1. A vital element in keeping the peace is our military establishment. Our arms must be mighty, ready for instant action, so that no potential aggressor may be tempted to risk his own destruction.

2. Our military organization today bears little relation to that known by any of my predecessors in peacetime, or indeed by the fighting men of World War II or Korea.

3   Until the latest of our world conflicts, the United States had no armaments industry. American makers of plowshares could, with time and as required, make swords as well. But now we can no longer risk emergency improvisation of national defense; we have been compelled to create a permanent armaments industry of vast proportions. Added to this, three and a half million men and women are directly engaged in the defense establishment. We annually spend on military security more than the net income of all United States corporations.

4   This conjunction of an immense military establishment and a large arms industry is new in the American experience. The total influence—economic, political, even spiritual—is felt in every city, every State house, every office of the Federal government. We recognize the imperative need for this development. Yet we must not fail to comprehend its grave implications. Our toil, resources and livelihood are all involved; so is the very structure of our society.

5   In the councils of government, we must guard against the acquisition of unwarranted influence, whether sought or unsought, by the military-industrial complex. The potential for the disastrous rise of misplaced power exists and will persist.

6   We must never let the weight of this combination endanger our liberties or democratic processes. We should take nothing for granted. Only an alert and knowledgeable citizenry can compel the proper meshing of the huge industrial and military machinery of defense with our peaceful methods and goals, so that security and liberty may prosper together.

7. Identify Presidents Roosevelt and Eisenhower's views of the US military by writing one answer choice letter in each of the appropriate columns. (**Note**: On the actual GED® test, you will click on each choice and "drag" it into position in the chart.)

Roosevelt	Eisenhower

   A. The military is almost large enough to begin conquering other nations.
   B. The military is not yet large enough to defend the nation and the world.
   C. The military is too large because its spending is out of control.
   D. The military is necessarily large but should be watched carefully.

8. What is an assumption about the United States in Roosevelt's speech?

   A. It was building arms to give to other nations.
   B. It was planning to stay out of other nations' conflicts.
   C. It was working to promote international peace.
   D. It was preparing for the likelihood of world war.

9. Based on the details in both speeches, what advice might Roosevelt and Eisenhower give to an incoming president?

   A. Maintain a large military operation.
   B. Keep the military out of world conflicts.
   C. Let voters decide how big the military should be.
   D. Build the world's most respected military.

10. What do the two presidents' speeches have in common?

    A. Both employ emotional language to sway listeners.
    B. Both use a formal style to communicate serious ideas.
    C. Both present evidence from experts to support their claims.
    D. Both aim at an audience likely to agree with the speakers.

11. Which idea from Eisenhower's speech supports his claim that the US military is a "vast" organization?

    A. The influence of the military is felt in every American home.
    B. Americans should worry about the military's rapidly expanding power.
    C. More was spent on the military than all corporate profits combined.
    D. The American public should be aware of the military's methods.

12. According to both speeches, which is the most valid reason for building and maintaining a strong military?

    A. to inspire fear in America's enemies
    B. to keep the peace in troubled cities
    C. to prepare for conflicts abroad
    D. to boost the failing economy

13. How does paragraph 3 of Eisenhower's speech build upon his claim in paragraph 2?

    A. It refutes the argument that the military's influence has grown.
    B. It illustrates the idea that the military's role has changed over time.
    C. It supports the point that maintaining a large military has risks.
    D. It proves the assertion that Americans should be wary of the military.

14. Which is relevant evidence in support of Roosevelt's claim that it is "no small task" to build up the US military?

    A. Factories, shipways, and other facilities had to be built first.
    B. Industry leaders joined the effort to make war equipment.
    C. Production of airplanes was far behind that of warships.
    D. American voters agreed on the need for building up the military.

PRETEST

15. What main idea can you infer from paragraphs 5–6 of Eisenhower's speech?

    A. Americans should seek out high-paying jobs with the military.
    B. Americans should welcome the expansion of the military in the world.
    C. Americans should vote against increasing spending on the military.
    D. Americans should be watchful as the influence of the military grows.

16. How does the word *therefore* in paragraph 7 of Roosevelt's speech help reinforce the president's purpose?

    A. It makes a connection between the voters' will and world peace.
    B. It provides a transition to the president's declaration of war.
    C. It shifts the speech from a discussion of policy to one of action.
    D. It signals a contrast with previous statements about the military.

17. Which claim made by Roosevelt lacks supporting evidence?

    A. Some of the goals for building military equipment have been met.
    B. The task of rebuilding the American military is huge.
    C. The United States has a policy for defending itself and the world.
    D. The American public is united in its support of the national policy.

Use the passage to answer Questions 18–22.

1   His name was George F. Babbitt. He was forty-six years old now, in April, 1920, and he made nothing in particular, neither butter nor shoes nor poetry, but he was nimble in the calling of selling houses for more than people could afford to pay.

2   His large head was pink, his brown hair thin and dry. His face was babyish in slumber, despite his wrinkles and the red spectacle-dents on the slopes of his nose. He was not fat but he was exceedingly well fed; his cheeks were pads, and the unroughened hand which lay helpless upon the khaki-colored blanket was slightly puffy. He seemed prosperous, extremely married and unromantic; and altogether unromantic appeared this sleeping-porch, which looked on one sizable elm, two respectable grass-plots, a cement driveway, and a corrugated iron garage. Yet Babbitt was again dreaming of the fairy child, a dream more romantic than scarlet pagodas by a silver sea.

3   For years the fairy child had come to him. Where others saw but Georgie Babbitt, she discerned gallant[1] youth. She waited for him, in the darkness beyond mysterious groves. When at last he could slip away from the crowded house he darted to her. His wife, his clamoring friends, sought to follow, but he escaped, the girl fleet beside him, and they crouched together on a shadowy hillside. She was so slim, so white, so eager! She cried that he was gay[2] and valiant, that she would wait for him, that they would sail—

---

[1] gallant: gentlemanly, heroic
[2] gay: joyful

4   Rumble and bang of the milk-truck.

5   Babbitt moaned; turned over; struggled back toward his dream. He could see only her face now, beyond misty waters. The furnace-man slammed the basement door. A dog barked in the next yard. As Babbitt sank blissfully into a dim warm tide, the paper-carrier went by whistling, and the rolled-up *Advocate* thumped the front door. Babbitt roused, his stomach constricted with alarm. As he relaxed, he was pierced by the familiar and irritating rattle of someone cranking a Ford:[3] snap-ah-ah, snap-ah-ah, snap-ah-ah. Himself a pious[4] motorist, Babbitt cranked with the unseen driver, with him waited through taut hours for the roar of the starting engine, with him agonized as the roar ceased and again began the infernal patient snap-ah-ah—a round, flat sound, a shivering cold-morning sound, a sound infuriating and inescapable. Not till the rising voice of the motor told him that the Ford was moving was he released from the panting tension. He glanced once at his favorite tree, elm twigs against the gold patina of sky, and fumbled for sleep as for a drug. He who had been a boy very credulous of life was no longer greatly interested in the possible and improbable adventures of each new day.

6   He escaped from reality till the alarm-clock rang, at seven-twenty.

18. Which word would be the *best* substitute for *nimble* in the first paragraph?

    A. alert
    B. graceful
    C. able
    D. lively

19. How would you describe Babbitt's relationship with the fairy child?

    A. sympathetic
    B. disagreeable
    C. casual
    D. fanciful

20. What is the role of the details in paragraphs 2 and 3?

    A. They illustrate parallels between Babbitt's real life and his dreams.
    B. They show the effect of Babbitt's real life on the actions in his dreams.
    C. They highlight the contrast between Babbitt's real life and his dreams.
    D. They describe a typical day in Babbitt's real life and in his dreams.

---

[3] cranking a Ford: old-fashioned way to start a car by turning a handle
[4] pious: devoted

PRETEST

Use the excerpt below to answer Question 21:

He who had been a boy very credulous of life was no longer greatly interested in the possible and improbable adventures of each new day.

21. Which word would change the tone and meaning of the sentence if it replaced *credulous*?

    A. frightened
    B. confident
    C. assured
    D. trusting

22. Which *best* describes this story's theme?

    A. the joy of married life
    B. the tragedy of growing older
    C. the danger of early success
    D. the desire to escape reality

THIS IS THE END OF PART 1. GO ON TO PART 2.

Part 2: Extended Response

1 question | **45 minutes**

Use the following two excerpts for Item 1.

Driverless Cars Are a Good Idea

Driverless cars are without a doubt safer and more convenient than the passenger cars driven today. Those who love innovation will love them. Those who don't crave new technology may still be won over by the cars' many positive features.

First, they are safer. These cars don't drink and drive; they can't fall asleep at the wheel; they won't text or experience road rage. The rates of traffic accidents and accident-related injuries or death are sure to drop.

Second, their convenience is unmatched. Especially in cities, a major reason that people avoid driving—besides traffic—is to avoid the hassle of parking. When a driverless car reaches its destination, the passenger gets out, and the car parks itself. The owner simply summons it by smartphone when he or she needs it again. In addition, these cars will give people more free time. The hours now wasted sitting in a car during a long commute could be time spent in leisure activities such as reading, viewing a film, or even catching up on sleep.

Most important, studies show that driverless cars are cheaper and better for the environment. Car ownership will likely decline in favor of car-sharing systems, such as Zipcar. Anyone can use a driverless car. That means others—family members or friends—may use your driverless car when you are at work. This ability to share resources cuts down on the need to purchase multiple vehicles and will ultimately lead to fewer vehicles on the road. According to a study by MIT, driverless cars will reduce congestion and pollution, especially in cities, because fewer vehicles will be on the road.

This is not the first time cars would profoundly affect society. Henry Ford's Model-T made passenger cars available to the average person, a change that revolutionized transportation. Driverless cars are a new revolution that meshes with modern wants and needs in many significant ways.

Let's Reverse the Trend toward a Driverless Society

Driverless cars are an interesting concept, but they will not be good for people, the economy, or the environment. No one is really sure how driverless cars will act. Although technological innovation is something we all want, driverless cars are machines still designed and made by humans; therefore, they will malfunction in unpredictable ways, just as regular cars do. The New Orleans Institute for Technological Studies notes that driverless cars are still in the experimental stage.

First, current tests reveal that a small percentage of driverless cars go off route, take wrong turns, or stop without warning. Riders will not have enough time to address these errors when they occur, especially if they are not paying attention, and accidents will result. Pedestrians will have to be more cautious than ever with these unpredictable vehicles cruising the streets.

In a survey conducted by the Alliance of Automobile Manufacturers, 42% said that driverless cars were a bad idea. Only 33% said it was a good idea, and 24% of the 2,000 adults surveyed did not know whether cars that can pilot themselves were good or bad. Of those surveyed, 86% answered that the person "operating" a driverless car should still have a driver's license.

Finally, some say that driverless cars are energy savers, but the opposite is more likely. The ease of driving will result in people choosing individual cars over public transportation. People will not mind driving much longer distances if they can spend their time doing something they enjoy. Increased urban congestion and pollution will be the result.

The driverless car sounds like a good idea on the surface, but it does not truly benefit the American public. We should concentrate on building better vehicles for today's drivers, not fantasy vehicles that will create more problems than solutions.

1. Extended response

Analyze both texts to determine which position is best supported. Use relevant and specific evidence from both sources to support your response.

12 PRETEST: Reasoning through Language Arts

PRETEST

Write or type your response on a separate page. This task may require approximately 45 minutes to complete.

THIS IS THE END OF PART 2. YOU MAY TAKE A 10-MINUTE BREAK.

PRETEST

Part 3

40 questions | **60 minutes**

*The following memo contains several numbered blanks, each marked "[Select... ▼]". Beneath each one is a set of choices. Indicate the choice from each set that is correct and belongs in the blank. (**Note**: On the real GED® test, the choices will appear as a "drop-down" menu. When you click on a choice, it will appear in the blank.)*

Memo

To: All Employees

From: Management Office

Re: Computer Problems

[1. Select... ▼] due to unresolved computer problems. This is an unfortunate outcome to what should be a relatively straightforward problem to fix. In an attempt to improve the situation, we are instituting a new system for dealing with technical issues.

1. Select... ▼
A. We has noticed that a lot of time has been lost
B. We have noticed that a lot of time have been lost
C. We has noticed that a lot of time have been lost
D. We have noticed that a lot of time has been lost

As of this notice, any employee who is experiencing a computer technical difficulty needs to contact Informational Technology directly by calling extension 361 rather than contacting the department through email. If you reach IT's answering machine, [2. Select... ▼] You will be contacted within three hours of your call. If that does not happen, call extension 256, and you will be connected with troubleshooting. That will ensure that an IT person returns your call.

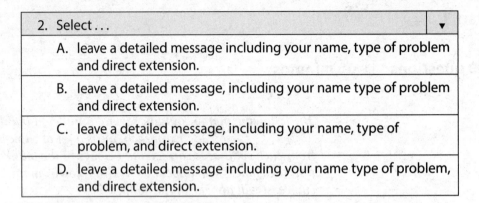

All problems will be dealt with in the order that they are reported. When the IT person calls you to discuss the problem, 3. Select... ▼ via the phone. If that does not work, an IT person will make an appointment to come to your work site.

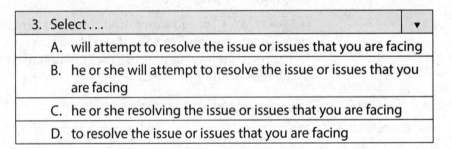

Be aware that because there is a limited IT staff, 4. Select... ▼ before an IT person will be available to work onsite. In the meantime, employees should keep a log of any work that could not be completed because of a computer issue.

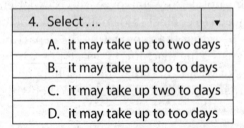

If a computer problem remains unresolved for more than a day, call 5. Select... ▼ at extension 65 to report that fact. You will be given a temporary work site with a different computer until the issue is successfully resolved. 6. Select... ▼

PRETEST

5. Select... ▼
A. ms. lopez in the Human Resources Department
B. Ms. Lopez in the Human Resources Department
C. Ms. lopez in the human resources department
D. ms. Lopez in the Human Resources department

6. Select... ▼
A. We hope that this new way of handling computer problems will be efficient and no work suffering as a result.
B. We hope this new way of handling computer problems be efficient and no work to suffer as a result.
C. We hope that this new way of handling computer problems will be efficient and that no work will suffer as a result.
D. We hope this new way of handling computer problems being efficient and that no work suffering as a result.

Use the passage to answer Questions 7–13.

Preventing Youth Violence

1   Youth violence results in considerable physical, emotional, social, and economic consequences. Although rates of youth homicide have declined substantially since the mid-1990s, much work remains in reducing this public health burden. Homicide remains a leading cause of death among youth aged 10–24 years in the United States. Violence is also a major cause of nonfatal injuries among youth. In 2011, more than 700,000 young people aged 10–24 years were treated in emergency departments for nonfatal injuries sustained from assaults.

2   It is wrong to blame youth violence on any one issue. The reality is that multiple factors influence whether or not youth violence occurs. These influences vary as children get older and the community around them changes.

   A young person's characteristics and experiences play an important role, and so do their relationships with friends and family and the characteristics of the community where they live.

3   Consider Jason, a 12-year-old boy whose mother works two jobs to support him and his older brother. Unemployment and drug abuse are common in their neighborhood. Because of bullying at school and the high crime rate in their neighborhood, Jason's brother has taught him to

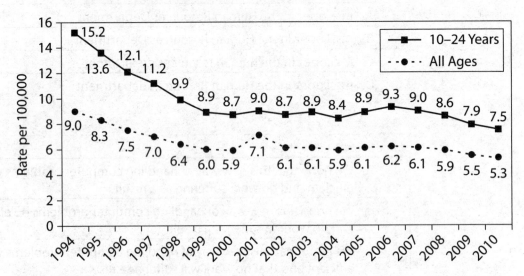

Violent Incidents Resulting in Injury (US Teens and General Population)

* Rates for all ages are age-adjusted to the standard 2000 population; rates for the 10–24 years age group are age-specific.

strike first to avoid being robbed or harassed. Jason and his friends have a reputation for being tough, and classmates are scared of them.

4 Even though Jason acts tough, he often feels afraid and doesn't know how to deal with his fear. After witnessing the shooting of a neighbor, he has nightmares and stomachaches that keep him awake at night. In school he feels restless and has trouble concentrating. Jason's school tries to meet the needs of its students, but with dwindling resources and increasing class sizes, the school is unable to give him all the extra help he needs. After school he is often home alone and has trouble doing his homework, so he keeps falling farther behind.

5 Then people in Jason's community came together and developed a comprehensive approach to preventing youth violence. Jason benefits from a new afterschool program that offers a safe environment and tutoring, he is connected with a trained mentor, and his school has started using an evidence-based violence prevention program. His brother gets support from a street outreach program. In addition, improvements in lighting, regular neighborhood cleanup, and activities to promote economic growth all sponsored by local businesses have Jason's family feeling safer and more optimistic about the future.

6 Kids like Jason have multiple influences that put them at risk—emotional and academic difficulties, friends who get in trouble, encouragement to be aggressive, limited adult supervision, exposure to community violence, and poverty. Fortunately, Jason also has many protective factors, including a caring family, a growing connection to neighborhood supports, and a community that is looking for ways to increase safety and prosperity.

PRETEST

Knowing the factors that put young people at risk helps us see the opportunities for preventing youth violence. We can do more for Jason and youth like him than just being prepared with the necessary police officers, prison cells, and hospital beds to deal with the aftermath of youth violence.

7   We can use proven approaches to address risk factors and increase protective factors. We can prevent youth violence before it happens. For example:

- **Universal School-based Youth Violence Prevention Programs** provide students and educators with information about violence and teach skills to nonviolently resolve disputes.

- **Parenting Skill and Family Relationship Approaches** provide caregivers with support and teach communication, problem solving, monitoring, and behavior-management skills.

- **Policy, Environmental, and Structural Approaches** involve changes to community environments that can enhance safety and reduce the risk for violence

[Adapted from http://www.cdc.gov/violenceprevention/youthviolence/pdf/Opportunities-for-Action-Companion-Guide.pdf]

7. How does the line graph relate to paragraph 1 of the text?

    A. It supports the claim that community action can cut youth violence.
    B. It extends the claim that many factors affect youth violence.
    C. It illustrates the claim that youth violence has been declining.
    D. It contradicts the claim about the frequency of youth violence.

8. How is the focus of the graph different from the text?

    A. The graph shows a steady gap between youth violence and all violent incidents since 1994; the text considers only youth violence.
    B. The graph tracks trends of youth violence over twenty years; the text emphasizes recent incidents of youth violence.
    C. The graph compares declines in youth violence to violence in the general population; the text focuses on how to reduce youth violence.
    D. The graph indicates that youth violence is an ongoing problem; the text suggests that the problem has largely been resolved.

9. What conclusion can you draw from reading the text and the graph?

    A. Youth violence is caused by many different factors and continues to rise.
    B. Youth violence remains at the same level, despite new programs to stop it.
    C. Youth violence can be prevented, but many communities refuse to try.
    D. Youth violence is declining but is higher than in the general population.

10. How does the structure of the passage support the author's purpose?

   A. The author tells one boy's story of youth violence and highlights some effective solutions.
   B. The author presents one community's problems with youth violence and suggests a step-by-step solution.
   C. The author identifies some general causes of youth violence and describes its effect on one family.
   D. The author considers the history of youth violence and describes its impact on schools.

11. What is the relationship between paragraph 6 and paragraphs 4–5?

   A. Paragraph 6 provides a solution to the problems noted in paragraphs 4–5.
   B. Paragraph 6 makes a generalization based on anecdotes in paragraphs 4–5.
   C. Paragraph 6 describes the effect of violence referred to in paragraphs 4–5.
   D. Paragraph 6 explains the downside of the actions taken in paragraphs 4–5.

12. Which sentence from the passage states the main idea?

   A. The people in Jason's community came together and developed a comprehensive approach to preventing youth violence.
   B. A young person's characteristics and experiences play an important role, and so do their relationships with friends and family.
   C. Even though Jason acts tough, he often feels afraid and doesn't know how to deal with his fear.
   D. Knowing the factors that put young people at risk helps us see the opportunities for preventing youth violence.

13. Identify two factors that the passage says can cause youth violence. Write the letters of your choices in the blank circles. (**Note**: On the actual GED test, you will click on an answer choice and "drag" it into position in the web.)

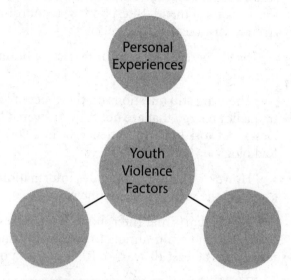

A. Relationships with family and friends
B. School class sizes
C. Community characteristics
D. Access to medical care

Use the passage to answer Questions 14–20.

Adapted from *Call 911* "Are Cell Phones a Danger to Your Health?"

1   Do the radio waves that cell phones emit pose a threat to health?

2   Although research is ongoing, the Food and Drug Administration (FDA) says that available scientific evidence—including World Health Organization (WHO) findings released May 17, 2010—shows no increased health risk due to radiofrequency (RF) energy, a form of electromagnetic radiation that is emitted by cell phones.

3   The FDA also cites a separate National Cancer Institute program finding that, despite the dramatic increase in cell phone use, occurrences of brain cancer did not increase between 1987 and 2005 . . . .

4   Although cell phones can be sold without FDA clearance or approval, the agency monitors the effects the phones have on health. The FDA has the

authority to take action if cell phones are shown to emit RF energy at a level that is hazardous to the user.

5   The findings released in May 2010 are from Interphone, a series of studies initiated in 2000 and conducted in 13 countries (the United States was not one of them). Interphone was coordinated by WHO's International Agency for Research on Cancer.

6   The study reported little or no risk of brain tumors for most long-term users of cell phones.

7   "There are still questions on the effect of long-term exposure to radio frequency energy that are not fully answered by Interphone," says Abiy Desta, network leader for science at the FDA's Center for Devices and Radiological Health.

8   "However, this study provides information that will be of great value in assessing the safety of cell phone use."

9   WHO reports that Interphone is the largest case-control study of cell phone use and brain tumors to date and includes the largest numbers of users, with at least 10 years of RF energy exposure.

10 The study focuses on four types of tumors found in the tissues that most absorb RF energy emitted by cell phones: tumors of the brain known as glioma and meningioma, of the acoustic nerve, and of the parotid gland (the largest of the salivary glands). The goal was to determine whether cell phone use increased the risk of developing these tumors.

11 The recent Interphone findings, which are being posted online in the June 2010 *International Journal of Epidemiology*, did not show an increased risk of brain cancer from using cell phones.

12 Although some of the data suggested an increased risk for people with the heaviest use of cell phones, the study's authors determined that biases and errors limit the strength of conclusions that can be drawn from it.

13 According to WHO, cell phone use has become much more prevalent, and it is not unusual for young people to use cell phones for an hour or more a day. This increasing use is tempered, however, by the lower emissions, on average, from newer technology phones and the increasing use of texting and hands-free operations that keep the phone away from the head.

14 Although evidence shows little or no risk of brain tumors for most long-term users of cell phones, the FDA says people who want to reduce their RF exposure can:

  • reduce the amount of time spent on the cell phone

  • use speaker mode or a headset to place more distance between the head and the cell phone

14. What is the author's primary purpose for writing the passage?

    A. to inform readers of the results of a study involving cell phones
    B. to persuade readers to use their cell phones with less frequency
    C. to describe for readers the effects of radiation on cell phone users
    D. to explain to readers why cell phones pose a risk of some cancers

Use the following excerpt to answer Question 15:

   Although research is ongoing, the Food and Drug Administration (FDA) says that available scientific evidence ... shows no increased health risk due to radiofrequency (RF) energy, a form of electromagnetic radiation that is emitted by cell phones.

15. What inference about cell phones can you make based on this sentence?

    A. People thought they might have negative health effects.
    B. They have been proven to be perfectly safe for daily use.
    C. The FDA is required to conduct studies on all new models.
    D. Exposure to their electromagnetic radiation is minimal.

16. Which is the *best* summary of paragraph 13?

    A. More young people have cell phones today, so it is important that they learn to use them carefully to avoid exposure to radiation.
    B. Young cell phone users who text and use headphones are less likely to be exposed to radiation and experience negative health effects.
    C. Young people spend time on their cell phones each day, but lower emissions and increased texting reduce their exposure to radiation.
    D. The World Health Organization study found that young cell phone users were unlikely to have much exposure to radiation.

17. Based on paragraph 7, what conclusion can you draw about the study?

    A. It failed to fully resolve all concerns about cell phones and cancer.
    B. It convinced cell phone makers to reduce the radiation in their products.
    C. It caused many consumers to reconsider the daily use of their cell phones.
    D. It reminded cell phone buyers that high-tech products come with risks.

18. What role do the details in the bulleted list play in this passage?

    A. They provide background information about the recent cell phone study.
    B. They sum up the author's key points about the risks of cell phone usage.
    C. They identify ways to reduce one's exposure to cell phone radiation.
    D. They list data about cell phones found by the World Health Organization.

PRETEST

19. What relationship exists between cell phone use and brain cancers?

    A. Cell phones ease those suffering from brain cancers.
    B. Cell phones pose little to no risk for brain cancers.
    C. Cell phones help scientists detect brain cancers.
    D. Cell phones cause certain kinds of brain cancers.

20. Identify two additional things that the FDA recommends to people who want to reduce RF exposure. Write the letters of your choices in the blank circles. (**Note:** On the actual GED test, you will click on an answer choice and "drag" it into position in the web.)

    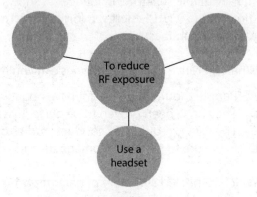

    A. Use a speakerphone.
    B. Use an RF-blocking cell phone case.
    C. Wear an ear guard.
    D. Spend less time talking on cell phones.

Use the passage to answer Questions 21–27.

Excerpt from the Inaugural Address of President John F. Kennedy (1961)

1   Let the word go forth from this time and place, to friend and foe alike, that the torch has been passed to a new generation of Americans—born in this century, tempered by war, disciplined by a hard and bitter peace, proud of our ancient heritage, and unwilling to witness or permit the slow undoing of those human rights to which this nation has always been committed, and to which we are committed today at home and around the world.

2   Let every nation know, whether it wishes us well or ill, that we shall pay any price, bear any burden, meet any hardship, support any friend, oppose any foe, to assure the survival and the success of liberty.

3   This much we pledge—and more.

4   To those old allies whose cultural and spiritual origins we share, we pledge the loyalty of faithful friends. United there is little we cannot do in a host of cooperative ventures. Divided there is little we can do—for we dare not meet a powerful challenge at odds and split asunder.

5   To those new states whom we welcome to the ranks of the free, we pledge our word that one form of colonial control shall not have passed away merely to be replaced by a far more iron tyranny. We shall not always expect to find them supporting our view. But we shall always hope to find them strongly supporting their own freedom—and to remember that, in the past, those who foolishly sought power by riding the back of the tiger ended up inside.

6   To those people in the huts and villages of half the globe struggling to break the bonds of mass misery, we pledge our best efforts to help them help themselves, for whatever period is required—not because the Communists may be doing it, not because we seek their votes, but because it is right. If a free society cannot help the many who are poor, it cannot save the few who are rich.

7   To our sister republics south of our border, we offer a special pledge: to convert our good words into good deeds, in a new alliance for progress, to assist free men and free governments in casting off the chains of poverty. But this peaceful revolution of hope cannot become the prey of hostile powers. Let all our neighbors know that we shall join with them to oppose aggression or subversion anywhere in the Americas. And let every other power know that this hemisphere intends to remain the master of its own house.

8   To that world assembly of sovereign states, the United Nations, our last best hope in an age where the instruments of war have far outpaced the instruments of peace, we renew our pledge of support—to prevent it from becoming merely a forum for invective, to strengthen its shield of the new and the weak, and to enlarge the area in which its writ may run.

9   Finally, to those nations who would make themselves our adversary, we offer not a pledge but a request: that both sides begin anew the quest for peace, before the dark powers of destruction unleashed by science engulf all humanity in planned or accidental self-destruction.

21. How do paragraphs 1-2 fit into the rest of Kennedy's speech?

    A. They state America's mission to support worldwide human rights.
    B. They outline plans to enlarge the military system within a year.
    C. They address America's enemies by threatening military action.
    D. They ask other nations to join the efforts to build world peace.

22. In paragraph 4, how does Kennedy distinguish his point of view from that of some "states we welcome to the ranks of the free"?

    A. by quoting their objections in his speech
    B. by encouraging them to consider his side
    C. by presenting facts to counter their opinions
    D. by acknowledging their different views

23. How does Kennedy communicate his ideas about freedom?

    A. He draws a parallel between pre-war United States and modern times.
    B. He lists the steps he wants to take toward building up the military.
    C. He aims his remarks directly to the world's nations and the United Nations.
    D. He repeats several times how his national policy had voters' full support.

24. What is Kennedy's implicit purpose for giving this speech?

    A. to ask the nations of the world to leave America alone
    B. to invite other nations to join America in a policy of peace
    C. to encourage other nations to support American military policy
    D. to warn the world's nations that America will defeat them in war

25. Which of the following is most likely to be Kennedy's opinion about the United Nations?

    A. It is too weak to be effective.
    B. It is comprised of nations that cannot agree on anything.
    C. It can strengthen and grow to be a real force for peace.
    D. It will expand to encompass all nations.

26. What does the word *tempered* mean as it is used in paragraph 1?

    A. angered
    B. strengthened
    C. damaged
    D. moderated

Use the following excerpt for question 27.

To those old allies whose cultural and spiritual origins we share, we pledge the loyalty of faithful friends.

27. Which of the following countries is most likely included in this description?

    A. Great Britain
    B. Mexico
    C. Russia
    D. China

Use the passage to answer Questions 28–34.

Excerpt from *A Little Princess* by Frances Hodges Burnett

1. "Here we are, Sara," said Captain Crewe, making his voice sound as cheerful as possible. Then he lifted her out of the cab and they mounted the steps and rang the bell. Sara often thought afterward that the house was somehow exactly like Miss Minchin. It was respectable and well furnished, but everything in it was ugly; and the very armchairs seemed to have hard bones in them. In the hall everything was hard and polished—even the red cheeks of the moon face on the tall clock in the corner had a severe varnished look. The drawing room into which they were ushered was covered by a carpet with a square pattern upon it, the chairs were square, and a heavy marble timepiece stood upon the heavy marble mantel.

2. As she sat down in one of the stiff mahogany chairs, Sara cast one of her quick looks about her.

3. "I don't like it, papa," she said. "But then I dare say soldiers—even brave ones—don't really LIKE going into battle."

4. Captain Crewe laughed outright at this. He was young and full of fun, and he never tired of hearing Sara's queer speeches.

5. "Oh, little Sara," he said. "What shall I do when I have no one to say solemn things to me? No one else is as solemn as you are."

6. "But why do solemn things make you laugh so?" inquired Sara.

7. "Because you are such fun when you say them," he answered, laughing still more. And then suddenly he swept her into his arms and kissed her very hard, stopping laughing all at once and looking almost as if tears had come into his eyes.

8. It was just then that Miss Minchin entered the room. She was very like her house, Sara felt: tall and dull, and respectable and ugly. She had large, cold, fishy eyes, and a large, cold, fishy smile. It spread itself into a very large smile when she saw Sara and Captain Crewe. She had heard a great many desirable things of the young soldier from the lady who had recommended her school to him. Among other things, she had heard that he was a rich father who was willing to spend a great deal of money on his little daughter.

9. "It will be a great privilege to have charge of such a beautiful and promising child, Captain Crewe," she said, taking Sara's hand and stroking it. "Lady Meredith has told me of her unusual cleverness. A clever child is a great treasure in an establishment like mine."

10   Sara stood quietly, with her eyes fixed upon Miss Minchin's face. She was thinking something odd, as usual.

11   "Why does she say I am a beautiful child?" she was thinking. "I am not beautiful at all. Colonel Grange's little girl, Isobel, is beautiful. She has dimples and rose-colored cheeks, and long hair the color of gold. I have short black hair and green eyes; besides which, I am a thin child and not fair in the least. I am one of the ugliest children I ever saw. She is beginning by telling a story."

12   She was mistaken, however, in thinking she was an ugly child. She was not in the least like Isobel Grange, who had been the beauty of the regiment,[5] but she had an odd charm of her own. She was a slim, supple creature, rather tall for her age, and had an intense, attractive little face. Her hair was heavy and quite black and only curled at the tips; her eyes were greenish gray, it is true, but they were big, wonderful eyes with long, black lashes, and though she herself did not like the color of them, many other people did. Still she was very firm in her belief that she was an ugly little girl, and she was not at all elated by Miss Minchin's flattery.

13   "I should be telling a story if I said she was beautiful," she thought; "and I should know I was telling a story. I believe I am as ugly as she is—in my way. What did she say that for?"

14   After she had known Miss Minchin longer she learned why she had said it. She discovered that she said the same thing to each papa and mamma who brought a child to her school.

28. Place the events of the story in the correct order by writing the appropriate answer choice in each of the boxes below. (**Note**: On the actual GED test, you will click on each answer choice and "drag" it into position in the chart.)

Order of Events

1.	
2.	
3.	
4.	

A. Sara questions Miss Minchin's intentions.
B. Miss Minchin compliments Sara.
C. Sara makes Captain Crewe laugh at one of her comments.
D. Captain Crewe and Sara enter Miss Minchin's school.

---

[5] regiment: an army unit

Use the excerpt below to answer Question 29:

[The room] was respectable and well furnished, but everything in it was ugly; and the very armchairs seemed to have hard bones in them. In the hall everything was hard and polished—even the red cheeks of the moon face on the tall clock in the corner had a severe varnished look.

29. What does the imagery in these sentences suggest about the setting?

    A. The room appears dark and gloomy.
    B. The room is quiet and book-filled.
    C. The room lacks comfort and ease.
    D. The room seems inviting and cozy.

30. Which of the following states a theme of the story?

    A. You should be honest with others and yourself.
    B. You should extend kindness to strangers in need.
    C. You should avoid judging others by appearances.
    D. You should ignore your first impressions of people.

31. Which word describes the relationship between Sara and Captain Crewe?

    A. convenient
    B. deceptive
    C. temporary
    D. affectionate

32. Based on the passage, what do you think will happen next to Sara?

    A. She will become Miss Minchin's favorite student.
    B. She will try to escape from Miss Minchin's school.
    C. She will appreciate Miss Minchin's storytelling ability.
    D. She will continue to distrust Miss Minchin's words.

Use the following line from paragraph 11 for question 33.

She is beginning by telling a story.

33. What does "telling a story" mean in this line?

    A. Miss Minchin wants to entertain Sara.
    B. Miss Minchin is lying.
    C. Miss Minchin is explaining about her school.
    D. Miss Minchin is being sarcastic.

34. Select any of the following words that describe Sara. Write an X on the blank for each of your choices. (**Note:** On the actual GED test, you will click next to each of your choices to put an X in the blank.)

_____	dark hair
_____	golden hair
_____	long hair
_____	short hair
_____	blue eyes
_____	green eyes
_____	thin
_____	dimples

The following letter contains several numbered blanks, each marked "Select...." Beneath each one is a set of choices. Indicate the choice from each set that is correct and belongs in the blank. (Note: On the real GED test, the choices will appear as a "drop-down" menu. When you click on a choice, it will appear in the blank.)

Dear Ms. Espinal,

We have reviewed your recent employment application and would like to further discuss opportunities within our company. We believe you are well qualified for the customer service representative position, [35. Select...▼] Everyone in this position works full time.

35. Select... ▼
A. which was currently available.
B. which has been currently available.
C. which is currently available.
D. which will be currently available.

Mr. Wong is the supervisor in this department. [36. Select...▼] Seldom do the representatives have problems in this department. The employees and Mr. Wong demonstrate positive attitudes, [37. Select...▼]

36. Select... ▼
A. The employees and he has built a strong working relationship.
B. The employees and him have built a strong working relationship.
C. The employees and he have built a strong working relationship.
D. They have built a strong working relationship.

PRETEST

37. Select... ▼
A. which creates an enjoyable work environment.
B. which create an enjoyable work environment.
C. which created an enjoyable work environment.
D. which create enjoyable work environments.

Customer service representatives at WINK, Inc., work five days each week, with weekends off. [38. Select... ▼], with a one-hour lunch break during the day. Anyone needing to adjust these hours due to appointments or emergencies [39. Select... ▼]

38. Select... ▼
A. We expect their employees to arrive promptly by 8:00 a.m. and to work until 5:00 p.m.
B. We expects our employees to arrive promptly by 8:00 a.m. and to work until 5:00 p.m.
C. We expect our employee to arrive promptly by 8:00 a.m. and to work until 5:00 p.m.
D. We expect our employees to arrive promptly by 8:00 a.m. and to work until 5:00 p.m.

39. Select... ▼
A. are able to do so occasionally.
B. is able to do so occasionally.
C. is being able to do so occasionally.
D. doing so occasionally.

We look forward to further discussing the customer service representative position with you. [40. Select... ▼]

40. Select... ▼
A. Thank you for your interested in working with our company.
B. Thank you for being interested in working at our company.
C. Thank you to be interested in working for our company.
D. Thank you for your interest in our company.

THIS IS THE END OF THE REASONING THROUGH LANGUAGE ARTS (RLA) PRETEST.

Answers and Explanations

Part 1:

1. Choice **D** correctly uses an apostrophe to indicate the possessive form.
2. Choice **A** correctly uses a conjunction to avoid a run-on sentence.
3. Choice **D** shows the correct subject–verb agreement.
4. Choice **B** shows the correct pronouns to refer to "a child."
5. Choice **C** correctly places the modifier after the word it modifies.
6. Choice **A** is correct. It uses a conjunctive adverb as a transition that makes sense given the meaning of the sentence.
7. Roosevelt's view is choice **B**. Eisenhower's is choice **D**.
8. Choice **D** is correct. Roosevelt wants to build up the military to deal with the outbreak of world war.
9. Choice **A** is correct. Both presidents talk about the need for a military to provide national defense and world peace.
10. Choice **B** is correct. Both use a formal style to convey ideas about the US military.
11. Choice **C** is the only fact directly related to the size of the military.
12. Choice **C** is correct. Both emphasize the need for the military to defend the United States and promote peace abroad.
13. Choice **B** is correct. The paragraph illustrates how the current military is different from the prewar military.
14. Choice **A** is correct. Before the military can be built up, factories and other structures must first be built. It is an enormous operation.
15. Choice **D** is correct. Eisenhower is warning Americans to be watchful of the influence of the military on daily and civic life.
16. Choice **C** is correct. It indicates a shift from policy to action.
17. Choice **D** is correct. The president provides no direct evidence to support this claim.
18. Choice **C** is correct. Babbitt is able to sell houses.
19. Choice **D** is correct. The fairy child is imaginary, or fanciful.
20. Choice **C** is correct. George's real life is full of noise and boring activities; his dreams are exciting and full of drama.
21. Choice **A** is correct. If Babbitt had been frightened of life, instead of credulous or believing, the meaning and tone of the sentence would change.
22. Choice **D** is correct. Babbitt dreams because he needs to escape reality.

Part 2:

If possible, ask an instructor to evaluate your essay. Your instructor's opinions and comments will help you determine what skills you need to practice to improve your writing skills. You may also want to evaluate your essay yourself, using the checklist that follows. The more items you can check, the more confident you can be about your writing skills. Items that are not checked will show you the essay-writing skills that you need to work on.

PRETEST

My essay:

- Creates a sound, logical argument based on the passage.
- Cites evidence from the passage to support the argument.
- Analyzes the issue and/or evaluates the validity of the arguments in the passage.
- Organizes ideas in a sensible sequence.
- Shows clear connections between main ideas.
- Uses largely correct sentence structure.
- Follows Standard English conventions in regard to grammar, spelling, and punctuation.

Part 3:

1. Choice **D** is correct. It shows subject–verb agreement.
2. Choice **C** correctly uses commas to set off clauses and items in a series.
3. Choice **B** is the only choice that does not create a sentence fragment.
4. Choice **A** correctly uses the homonyms *to* and *two*.
5. Choice **B** uses the correct capitalization.
6. Choice **C** is the only choice that uses proper parallel construction.
7. Choice **C** is correct. Paragraph 1 and the graph support the claim that youth violence has been declining since the mid-1990s.
8. Choice **C** is correct. The graph compares declines in youth violence to violence in the general population; the text focuses on how to reduce youth violence.
9. Choice **D** is correct. Youth violence is a problem that is declining, but youth violence remains higher than violence in the general population.
10. Choice **A** is correct. The author tells Jason's story as a way to personalize the problem of youth violence.
11. Choice **B** is correct. Paragraph 6 makes a generalization about the solutions to youth violence, drawing on Jason's experiences, described in paragraphs 4–5.
12. Choice **D** is correct. It states a main idea that covers the problem of youth violence and the fact that it can be prevented.
13. Choices **A** and **C** are correct. Relationships and community characteristics are influencing factors on youth violence.
14. Choice **A** is correct. The author's purpose is to inform readers.
15. Choice **A** is correct. The study was needed because people were worried.
16. Choice **C** covers all the key points in the correct order.
17. Choice **A** is correct. The FDA spokesperson says, "There are still questions to the effect of long-term exposure" to cell phone radiation.
18. Choice **C** is correct. The bulleted information identifies ways to reduce one's exposure to cell phone radiation.
19. Choice **B** is correct. There is no proven relationship between cell phones and brain cancers.
20. Choices **A** and **D** are correct. In paragraph 14, in addition the options already on the web, the FDA recommends that people who want to reduce RF exposure reduce time spent on cell phones or use speakerphone.
21. Choice **A** is correct. The paragraphs state America's human rights mission.
22. Choice **D** is correct. The president says, "We shall not always expect to find them supporting of our view."

PRETEST

23. Choice **C** is correct. Much of Kennedy's speech is addressed to other nations.

24. Choice **B** is correct. Kennedy addresses other nations and invites their cooperation.

25. Choice **C** is correct. In paragraph 8, Kennedy calls the United Nations "our last best hope," renews a pledge to support the UN and wishes that it be strengthened and expanded.

26. Choice **B** is correct. The word *tempered* means strengthened.

27. Choice **A** is correct. The quote says that we share cultural and spiritual origins. The only country listed in the answer choices that fits that description is Great Britain.

28. The correct order of events is **D, C, B, A**.

29. Choice **C** is correct. The chair's "hard bones" and the clock face's "varnished look" suggest a hard and shiny and uninviting room.

30. Choice **A** is correct. Sara is straightforward; Miss Minchin is a "storyteller." The story's theme is likely to center on honesty.

31. Choice **D** is correct. The father-daughter relationship is loving.

32. Choice **D** is correct. Sara will likely continue to value honesty over "storytelling."

33. Choice **B** is correct. "Telling a story" means Sara thinks Miss Minchin is lying.

34. You should have chosen: **short hair**, **dark hair**, **green eyes**, and **thin**. Sara's description is in paragraphs 11 and 12.

35. Choice **C** correctly uses the present tense verb.

36. Choice **C** correctly uses the subject pronoun *he* and the plural verb *have* matches the compound subject.

37. Choice **A** correctly uses the present tense singular verb *creates* because the subject *which* refers to the demonstration.

38. Choice **D** correctly uses the plural verb *expect* with the plural subject *we*, the possessive pronoun *our*, and the plural *employees*.

39. Choice **B** correctly uses the singular verb to agree with the singular subject *anyone*. Choice C also does this but is unnecessarily wordy.

40. Choice **D** uses the correct idiomatic expression *interest in* and is concise.

PRETEST

Evaluation Chart

Circle the item number of each item you missed. In the left column, you will find the names of the chapters that cover the skills you need to improve. More numbers circled in any row means more attention is needed to sharpen those skills for the GED® Test.

Chapter	Part 1 Questions	Part 3 Questions
Chapter 1: Grammar and Conventions	1, 2, 3, 4, 5, 6	1, 2, 3, 4, 5, 6, 35, 36, 37, 38, 39, 40
Chapter 2: Informational Texts	n/a	7, 8, 9, 10, 11, 12, 13, 14, 15, 16, 17, 18, 19, 20
Chapter 3: Argumentation and Persuasion	7, 8, 9, 10, 11, 12, 13, 14, 15, 16, 17	21, 22, 23, 24, 25, 26, 27
Chapter 4: Literature	18, 19, 20, 21, 22	28, 29, 30, 31, 32, 33, 34

If you find you need instruction before you are ready to practice your skills with this workbook, we offer several excellent options:

McGraw-Hill Education Preparation for the GED Test: This book contains a complete test preparation program with intensive review and practice for the topics tested on the GED.

McGraw-Hill Education Pre-GED: This book is a beginner's guide for students who need to develop a solid foundation or refresh basic skills before they embark on formal preparation for the GED test.

McGraw-Hill Education Short Course for the GED: This book provides a concise review of all the essential topics on the GED, with numerous additional practice questions.

CHAPTER 1
Grammar and Conventions

The following memo from the manager of an apartment complex contains several numbered blanks, each marked "[Select... ▼]" Beneath each one is a set of choices. Indicate the choice from each set that is correct and belongs in the blank. (**Note**: *On the real GED® test, the choices will appear as a "drop-down" menu. When you click on a choice, it will appear in the blank.*)

To: All Residents

From: Manager, Lodge Apartments

Subject: Community Garden

Date: April 7, 20XX

To promote the health and well-being of our residents, we are pleased to offer all tenants the use of a new community garden on the apartment complex premises behind Building 25. If you wish to participate in the community garden, please sign up in the manager's office no later than 5 p.m. on April 30.

How Do I Start?

You will be assigned a plot of land of approximately 49 square feet in the community garden. Our maintenance staff at the apartment complex will help till the plots for your garden during the first week of May. Management will contact you when maintenance has completed digging your garden plot. You may start planting right away.

You will be responsible for providing [1. Select... ▼] It is important to follow these [2. Select... ▼]

1. Select... ▼
A. your own seeds, additional soil bucket and gardening tools.
B. your own seeds; additional soil bucket, and gardening tools.
C. your own seeds, additional soil, a bucket, and gardening tools.
D. your own seeds, additional soil, a bucket and gardening tools.

35

2. Select... ▼
A. community rules. If you do not, you will lose your gardening privileges.
B. community rules! If you do not, you will lose your gardening privileges!!
C. community rules? if you do not, you will lose your gardening privileges?
D. community rules, if you do not, you will lose your gardening privileges.

Who Can Use It?

The garden is only available to renters and their family members who live in the complex, not to visiting friends or relatives. We encourage children to participate in the community garden project, but they must be under adult supervision at all times. The garden offers many learning opportunities, making 3. Select... ▼

3. Select... ▼
A. one a great educational resource for children.
B. them a great educational resource for children.
C. he or she a great educational resource for children.
D. it a great educational resource for children.

Who Takes Care of It?

You must plant your garden by June 1, or you will lose the plot reserved for you. Do not neglect your garden.

Keep your plot free of weeds, and otherwise tend your garden 4. Select... ▼ You must avoid using any herbicides or chemical pesticides to keep the garden safe for you and your neighbors. In addition, be sure to harvest your garden in a timely manner, so that vegetables, fruits, and flowers do not rot or go to waste.

4. Select... ▼
A. so that it does not interfere with anyone elses.
B. so that it does not interfere with anyone elses'.
C. so that it does not interfere with anyone else's.
D. so that it does not interfere with anyone's else.

Nothing compares to eating fresh produce or picking flowers that you have grown yourself.

Lodge Apartments is pleased to offer our residents the chance to
[5. Select... ▼]

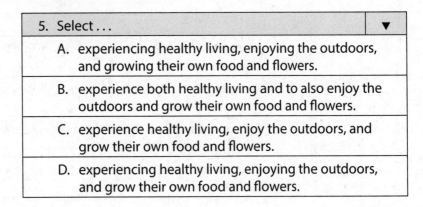

5. Select...	▼
A. experiencing healthy living, enjoying the outdoors, and growing their own food and flowers.	
B. experience both healthy living and to also enjoy the outdoors and grow their own food and flowers.	
C. experience healthy living, enjoy the outdoors, and grow their own food and flowers.	
D. experiencing healthy living, enjoying the outdoors, and grow their own food and flowers.	

*The following brochure from an animal shelter contains several numbered blanks, each marked "[Select... ▼]" Beneath each one is a set of choices. Indicate the choice from each set that is correct and belongs in the blank. (**Note**: On the real GED® test, the choices will appear as a "drop-down" menu. When you click on a choice, it will appear in the blank.)*

Adopt an Animal from the Barstock Animal Shelter Today!

Every year, thousands of dogs and cats are abused or abandoned by their owners. Left without food or shelter, these animals become sick and even die. In addition, most are not spayed or neutered, so they can produce litters of puppies and kittens that will also be without a home. This creates a vicious cycle.

[6. Select... ▼] The pet adoption process is inexpensive and convenient. When you adopt a pet, everybody wins!

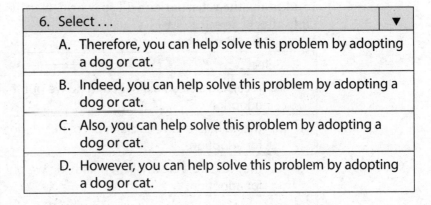

6. Select...	▼
A. Therefore, you can help solve this problem by adopting a dog or cat.	
B. Indeed, you can help solve this problem by adopting a dog or cat.	
C. Also, you can help solve this problem by adopting a dog or cat.	
D. However, you can help solve this problem by adopting a dog or cat.	

Benefits

Studies have repeatedly shown how beneficial pets are. Cats and dogs make wonderful companions, can lower blood pressure, and even alleviate depression and anxiety.

7. Select... ▼ The animal benefits, too, because by providing a loving home, you 8. Select... ▼

7. Select... ▼
A. Many children first learn to be responsible by caring for a beloved pet.
B. By caring for a beloved pet, many children learn to be responsible first.
C. First, by caring for a beloved pet, many children learn to be responsible.
D. To learn to be responsible first, many children care for a beloved pet.

8. Select... ▼
A. extend the animal's life span and stop the cycle of homelessness, you also make the world a better place.
B. extend the animal's life span and stop the cycle of homelessness and make the world a better place.
C. extend the animal's life span and stop the cycle of homelessness. You also make the world a better place.
D. extend the animal's life span and stop the cycle of homelessness, and therefore you also make the world a better place.

What We Do

The Barstock Animal Shelter provides several important services at no cost before you even choose your pet. An animal behaviorist evaluates each of our animals to assess any behavioral problems. Each animal also receives a full medical examination and rabies vaccination by a licensed veterinarian. In addition, the veterinarian will spay or neuter the animal, if necessary. Only after 9. Select... ▼

9. Select... ▼
A. receiving a clean bill of health do we put them up for adoption.
B. the animal receives a clean bill of health do we put it up for adoption.
C. they receive a clean bill of health, do we put them up for adoption.
D. the vet gives a clean bill of health, do we put him or her up for adoption.

10. Select... ▼ Before you visit the animals, a pet adoption counselor will have you fill out an application to help match you with the right pet. The questions asked, for example, are: Do you have small children? Do you prefer a quieter pet or a more active one? Would you like a younger or an older pet?

10. Select... ▼
A. The Shelter Is Open Tuesday Through Sunday From 10 a.m. to 6 p.m.
B. The shelter is Open tuesday through sunday from 10 a.m. to 6 p.m.
C. The Shelter is open Tuesday through sunday from 10 a.m. to 6 p.m.
D. The shelter is open Tuesday through Sunday from 10 a.m. to 6 p.m.

The most important 11. Select... ▼

11. Select... ▼
A. part of this process is taking a small amount of time to find the animal that is absolutely right for you, so you and your new pet can get started on a great life together as a team.
B. part of the adoption process is taking time to find the animal that is right for you, so you and your new pet can start a great life together.
C. part of the easy-to-do adoption process is taking just a few minutes of your time to find the animal that is totally right on target for you, so you and your new pet can start a great life of adventure together.
D. part of the process is finding the animal that is a perfectly good fit with you, so you two can get started right away on a wonderfully great life together.

*The following letter from a job applicant contains several numbered blanks, each marked "Select... ▼" Beneath each one is a set of choices. Indicate the choice from each set that is correct and belongs in the blank. (**Note**: On the real GED® test, the choices will appear as a "drop-down" menu. When you click on a choice, it will appear in the blank.)*

Mr. Ron Karpinski, Graphics Supervisor

Creative Solutions Graphics

300 Marvel Way

Seattle, WA 45896

Dear Mr. Karpinski:

My current employer, Mr. Clay Lamond, suggested that I [12. Select... ▼] Mr. Lamond is retiring at the end of the year and his company, MegaGraphics, will be closing, but he feels that my talents would be of great use to you.

12. Select... ▼
A. check in with you about a spot in the IT department at your place.
B. contact you about a possible employment opportunity in the Information Technology department at your firm.
C. drop a line to you about a job in the Information Technology department of your company.
D. shoot you a letter to pick your brain about working in your IT department.

I have a proven track record as a graphics designer with MegaGraphics. I began there as an intern in 2010, after graduating with honors from the University of Washington, Seattle.

Due to my excellent work, productivity, and reliability, [13. Select... ▼] As a graphics designer, I created logos and promotional materials, and I designed social media campaigns for several clients to establish their brands. My work repeatedly produced successful results.

13. Select... ▼
A. Mr. Lamond promoted myself to a full-time position in 2011.
B. Mr. Lamond promoted I to a full-time position in 2011.
C. Mr. Lamond promoted me to a full-time position in 2011.
D. Mr. Lamond promoted one to a full-time position in 2011.

14. Select... ▼ All of my clients expressed satisfaction with my work, citing my ability to think quickly, listen closely, and create unique work. I am happy to provide references from several of these clients.

14. Select... ▼
A. Two of my logos went on to win national awards.
B. To of my logos went on two win national awards.
C. Too of my logos went on too win national awards.
D. Two of my logos went on too win national awards.

15. Select... ▼ I welcome the opportunity to work for you and am sure Creative Solutions Graphics would benefit strongly from my talents. 16. Select... ▼ I look forward to hearing from you. Thank you for your time.

15. Select... ▼
A. Because it is known for its innovative approach, I have long admired your company.
B. I, known for its innovative approach to graphic design, have long admired your company.
C. I have long admired your company, which is known for its innovative approach to graphic design.
D. Known for its innovative approach to graphic design, I have long admired your company.

16. Select... ▼
A. I have both attached my résumé but also included samples of my work.
B. I have not only attached my résumé but included samples of my work.
C. I have attached my résumé and furthermore included samples of my work.
D. I have attached my résumé and also included samples of my work.

Sincerely,

Luis La Hoya

*The following memorandum from a company's Human Resources Department contains several numbered blanks, each marked "Select... ▼" Beneath each one is a set of choices. Indicate the choice from each set that is correct and belongs in the blank. (**Note**: On the real GED® test, the choices will appear as a "drop-down" menu. When you click on a choice, it will appear in the blank.)*

Memorandum

To: All employees

From: Human Resources

Subject: Establishing flextime schedules

Date: October 1, 20XX

The Human Resources Department is excited to announce a change in how our company schedules employee work hours.

[17. Select... ▼] What is a flextime schedule? Employees at most companies work 9 a.m. to 5 p.m. each day. With flextime, employees may work from 7 a.m. to 3 p.m., 8 a.m. to 4 p.m., 9 a.m. to 5 p.m., or 10 a.m. to 6 p.m. The choice is up to the employee in conjunction with his or her supervisor. By October 31, all employees must meet with their supervisors and decide which schedule they will work.

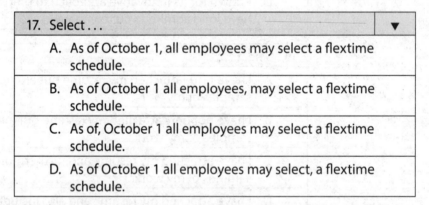

17. Select... ▼
A. As of October 1, all employees may select a flextime schedule.
B. As of October 1 all employees, may select a flextime schedule.
C. As of, October 1 all employees may select a flextime schedule.
D. As of October 1 all employees may select, a flextime schedule.

This schedule will remain in place for one year and cannot [18. Select... ▼]

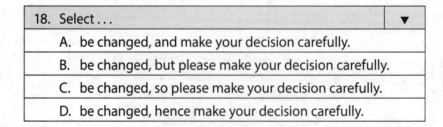

18. Select... ▼
A. be changed, and make your decision carefully.
B. be changed, but please make your decision carefully.
C. be changed, so please make your decision carefully.
D. be changed, hence make your decision carefully.

Flextime provides several benefits for employees. [19. Select...▼]. [20. Select...▼] For example, an employee with school-age children might prefer to finish work by 3 p.m.

19. Select... ▼
A. First, not everyone is at their best between 8 a.m. and 5 p.m.
B. First, not everyone is at his or her best between 8 a.m. and 5 p.m.
C. First, not everyone is at one's best between 8 a.m. and 5 p.m.
D. First, not everyone is at his best between 8 a.m. and 5 p.m.

20. Select... ▼
A. Some people do their best work early in the day, others prefer to avoid an early start because their energy peaks later in the day, still others have busy lives outside the office.
B. Some people do their best work early in the day, while others prefer to avoid an early start because their energy peaks later in the day, but still others have busy lives outside the office.
C. Some people do their best work early in the day, while others prefer to avoid an early start because their energy peaks later in the day. Still others have busy lives outside the office.
D. Some people do their best work early in the day, others prefer to avoid an early start because their energy peaks later in the day; meanwhile still others have busy lives outside the office.

Flextime also benefits the company. Studies show that employees who can define their working hours [21. Select...▼] placed a higher degree of trust in them. As a result, they feel more invested in their workplace, and their job performance improves.

21. Select... ▼
A. feel that their companies have
B. feels that their companies have
C. feels that their companies has
D. feel that their companies has

All employees [22. Select...▼] to discuss the flextime option. Supervisors will need time to fill out paperwork verifying the change for each employee in their division. Please direct any further questions to Human Resources.

22. Select... ▼
A. a meeting as soon as possible with their supervisors
B. schedule a meeting as soon as possible with their supervisors
C. as soon as possible schedule with their supervisors
D. must schedule a meeting as soon as possible with their supervisors

*The following letter from a consumer to a grocery chain contains several numbered blanks, each marked "[Select...▼]" Beneath each one is a set of choices. Indicate the choice from each set that is correct and belongs in the blank. (**Note**: On the real GED® test, the choices will appear as a "drop-down" menu. When you click on a choice, it will appear in the blank.)*

Ms. Donna Moore, Manager

Top Shelf Foods

2115 Blanchard Street

Cleveland, Ohio 95621

Dear Ms. Moore:

I am writing to complain about a recent development I noticed in my local Top Shelf Foods grocery store.

When I shop in a grocery store, I expect to have reasonable choices. I am spending my money [23. Select...▼] For example, I appreciate the fact that Top Shelf Foods offers its own less expensive line of canned and frozen foods, cleaning supplies, and other items. These may all save me money; however, sometimes I may prefer to buy a national brand due to the flavor or quality, even if it costs more. The choice [24. Select...▼]

23. Select... ▼
A. in that establishment; finally, I expect to make purchases based on my personal preferences.
B. in that establishment; similarly, I expect to be able to make purchases based on my personal preferences.
C. in that establishment; however, I expect to be able to make purchases based on my personal preferences.
D. in that establishment; therefore, I expect to be able to make purchases based on my personal preferences.

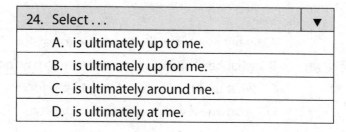

Lately, I have noticed that Top Shelf Foods is pushing its own brand of products very aggressively. There are fewer sales on national brands, which makes your brand an even more economical choice than usual. This is not unreasonable. However, what really bothers me 25. Select... ▼ In fact, they are gradually being replaced 26. Select... ▼ I used to have a choice between several brands of cereal and yogurt. Now there are only two: a national brand and the Top Shelf Foods house brand.

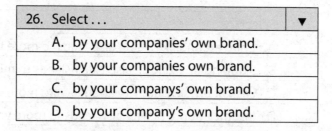

26. Select... ▼	
A.	by your companies' own brand.
B.	by your companies own brand.
C.	by your companys' own brand.
D.	by your company's own brand.

27. Select... ▼ This seems like a sneaky way to force me to buy your products. I understand that it is a good business practice to promote your own products. However, it should be up to the consumer to decide 28. Select... ▼

By depriving me of choices, Top Shelf Foods is driving me away as a customer.

27. Select... ▼	
A.	Soon there may be no choice at all.
B.	Soon their may be know choice at all.
C.	Soon their may be no choice at all.
D.	Soon there may be know choice at all.

28. Select... ▼
A. what they are willing and able to pay for.
B. what he or she is willing and able to pay for.
C. what they is willing and able to pay for.
D. what one is willing and able to pay for.

Sincerely,

Michael Smith

*The following brochure about how exercise affects heart health contains several numbered blanks, each marked "Select... ▼" Beneath each one is a set of choices. Indicate the choice from each set that is correct and belongs in the blank. (**Note**: On the real GED® test, the choices will appear as a "drop-down" menu. When you click on a choice, it will appear in the blank.)*

Exercise Is the Key to Heart Health

According to the US Surgeon General's Report on Physical Activity and Health, inactive people are nearly twice as likely to develop heart disease as those who are more active. This is true even if you have no other conditions or habits that increase your risk for heart disease. 29. Select... ▼ , more hospitalizations, and more use of medicines for a variety of illnesses. But most people do not get enough exercise. 30. Select... ▼

29. Select... ▼
A. Lying around like a slug also leads to more trips to the doctor
B. Skipping on exercise also totally leads to more runs to the ER
C. Lack of physical activity also leads to more visits to the doctor
D. Insufficient physicality also leads to more voyages to the doctor

30. Select... ▼
A. Fully 16 percent of Americans not active at all.
B. Fully 16 percent of Americans active not at all.
C. Fully 16 percent of Americans are not active at all.
D. Fully 16 percent of Americans never active at all.

The good news 31. Select... ▼ in a number of important ways.

31. Select... ▼
A. are that physical activity protects your heart
B. is that physical activity protect your heart
C. are that physical activity protect your heart
D. is that physical activity protects your heart

Moreover, to get benefits, you don't have to run a marathon. Regular activity—something as simple as a brisk, 30-minute walk each day—can help you reduce your risk of heart disease.

If you currently get regular physical activity, congratulations! However, if you're not yet getting all the activity you need, you have lots of company. According to the Centers for Disease Control and Prevention (CDC), 60 percent of Americans are not meeting the recommended levels of physical activity.

Overall, women tend to be less active than men, and older people are less likely to get regular physical activity than are younger individuals.

What does it mean to get "regular physical activity"? To reduce the risk of heart disease, adults need to do only about 30 minutes of moderate activity on most, and preferably all, days of the week. This level of activity can also lower your chances of 32. Select... ▼ If you're also trying to manage your weight and prevent gradual, unhealthy weight gain, try to get 60 minutes of moderate-to-vigorous-intensity activity on most days of the week. At the same time, watch your calories. 33. Select... ▼

32. Select... ▼
A. a stroke, colon cancer high blood pressure, and other medical problems.
B. a stroke, colon cancer, high blood pressure, and other medical problems.
C. a stroke colon cancer high blood pressure and other medical problems.
D. a stroke, colon cancer, high blood pressure, and other, medical problems.

33. Select... ▼
A. Take in only enough calories to maintain you're weight.
B. Take in only enough calories to maintain your wait.
C. Take in only enough calories to maintain your weight.
D. Take in only enough calories to maintain yours wait.

Those who are trying to keep weight off should aim a bit higher: Try to get 60–90 minutes of moderate-intensity activity daily, without taking in extra calories.

If you're not as active as you might be, take a moment to consider why. Maybe you're just in the habit of traveling by car or bus, even when you're not going far. In your free time, perhaps it's tempting to sit down in front of the TV or computer rather than do something more vigorous. It's easy to get busy or tired and decide that it's just simpler to put off that brisk walk or bike ride.

[34. Select...▼] physical inactivity can create for your health and the enormous rewards of regular exercise, you may want to reconsider.

34. Select... ▼
A. And when you think about the serious problems that
B. Plus when you think about the serious problems that
C. Thus when you think about the serious problems that
D. However, when you think about the serious problems that

*The following flyer announcing the opening of a community center contains several numbered blanks, each marked "[Select...▼]" Beneath each one is a set of choices. Indicate the choice from each set that is correct and belongs in the blank. (**Note**: On the real GED® test, the choices will appear as a "drop-down" menu. When you click on a choice, it will appear in the blank.)*

Announcing the Opening of the Maya Angelou Community Center!

The new Maya Angelou Community Center will open on June 15, 20XX.

[35. Select...▼] the Center will provide a wide range of exciting programs, classes, and activities for children aged 3–12.

35. Select... ▼
A. Located at the corner of Madison and Longview,
B. Located at the corner of madison and longview,
C. located at the Corner of Madison and Longview,
D. located at the corner of Madison and Longview

We Make Exercise Fun!

A New Playground: Behind the Center is a new playground built to safety standards. The playground includes a sandbox, a wading pool, slides, jungle gyms, and other equipment to invite play while improving fitness. Two monitors are always on hand [36. Select... ▼]

36. Select... ▼
A. to ensure children's safety.
B. to ensure childrens' safety.
C. to ensure children safety.
D. to ensure childrens's safety

However, children under age 7 must be accompanied by an adult. Comfortable benches have been installed in the playground so that parents or babysitters may observe their children.

A New Gymnasium: Our new indoor gym provides additional space for kids to play basketball or volleyball or participate in other sports. Two coaches are on the premises at all times to assist the children and to maintain safety. Again, we have provided seating for parents and babysitters to accompany their children. [37. Select... ▼]

37. Select... ▼
A. Come cheer them on?
B. Come cheer them on!
C. Come cheer them on;
D. Come cheer them on,

Exercise Classes for Kids: The Center will also offer low-cost exercise classes for children, such as karate, gymnastics, swimming, and dance. Classes last from 6–8 weeks and take place at various times during the day and into the evening. Some classes are restricted to specific ages. You may read class descriptions and age restrictions and sign your child up for a class by visiting www.macc.com/exerciseclass.

Let's Encourage Learning!

A New Playroom: The Center also includes a large, new playroom that children may use during inclement weather or when they prefer to do arts and crafts or other indoor activities. The room is stocked with board games and educational toys to stimulate children's minds, as well as art supplies to encourage creativity.

Educational Classes for Kids: The Center will offer educational classes about topics suited to children's ages and interests, including [38. Select...▼] Some classes take place one time only, while others last over a period of weeks. You may read class descriptions and sign your child up for classes at www.macc.com/educationalclass.

38. Select... ▼
A. how to build robots and go-carts, cooking, and finger painting.
B. to build robots and go-carts, cooking, and finger paints.
C. building robots and go-carts, cooking, and finger painting.
D. robots and go-carts, how to cook, and how to finger paint.

Come to Our Open House! Everyone Is Invited!

We are having an open house this Saturday, [39. Select...▼] Come to our new location at 7505 Longview Avenue from 2–6 p.m. Children are welcome to attend! Tour the new facility. Try out the new playground. Meet our staff. Join us as we paint a new mural in the playroom. [40. Select...▼]

39. Select... ▼
A. June 17, everyone in the neighborhood is invited!
B. June 17, and everyone in the neighborhood is invited!
C. June 17, Everyone in the neighborhood is invited!
D. June 17 because everyone in the neighborhood is invited!

40. Select... ▼
A. Will offer free drinks and refreshments during the open house.
B. Free drinks and refreshments on offer during the open house.
C. During the open house, free drinks and refreshments.
D. We will offer free drinks and refreshments during the open house.

CHAPTER 2
Informational Texts

Use the passage to answer Questions 1–8.

NASA-Developed Exoskeleton Can Help Astronauts and Paraplegics

1. Marvel Comic's fictional superhero, Ironman, uses a powered armor suit that allows him superhuman strength. While NASA's X1 robotic exoskeleton can't do what you see in the movies, the latest robotic space technology . . . may someday help astronauts stay healthier in space with the added benefit of assisting paraplegics in walking here on Earth.

2. NASA and the Institute for Human and Machine Cognition (IHMC) of Pensacola, Florida, with the help of engineers from Oceaneering Space Systems of Houston, have jointly developed a robotic exoskeleton called X1. The 57-pound device is a robot that a human could wear over his or her body, either to assist or inhibit movement in the leg joints.

3. In the inhibit mode, the robotic device would be used as an in-space exercise machine to supply resistance against leg movement. The same technology could be used in reverse on the ground, potentially helping some individuals walk for the first time.

4. Worn over the legs with a harness that reaches up the back and around the shoulders, X1 has 10 degrees of freedom, or joints—four motorized joints at the hips and the knees, and six passive joints that allow for sidestepping, turning and pointing, and flexing a foot. There also are multiple adjustment points, allowing the X1 to be used in many different ways.

5. NASA is examining the potential for the X1 as an exercise device to improve crew health both aboard the space station and during future long-duration missions to an asteroid or Mars. Without taking up valuable space or weight during missions, X1 could replicate common crew exercises, which are vital to keeping astronauts healthy in microgravity.[1] In addition, the device has the ability to measure, record, and stream back, in real time, data to flight controllers on Earth, giving doctors better feedback on the impact of the crew's exercise regimen.

6. Here on Earth, IHMC is interested in developing and using X1 as an assistive walking device. . . . X1 has the potential to allow for assisted walking over varied terrain, as well as stair climbing.

---

[1] microgravity: weak gravity

7 The potential of X1 extends to other applications, including rehabilitation, gait modification, and offloading[2] large amounts of weight from the wearer. Preliminary studies by IHMC have shown X1 to be more comfortable, easier to adjust, and easier to put on than previous exoskeleton devices. Researchers plan on improving on the X1 design, adding more active joints to areas, such as the ankle and hip, which will in turn increase the potential uses for the device.

1. According to paragraphs 1 and 2, what is the author's primary purpose?

   A. to encourage people to become interested in robotics
   B. to discuss how the X1 improves travel in outer space
   C. to persuade the government to support NASA's programs
   D. to show how scientific inventions may have a variety of uses

2. What inference can you make about the X-1 based on the details in paragraph 4?

   A. It is a heavy device.
   B. It is a complex device.
   C. It is a dangerous device.
   D. It is a costly device.

3. Indicate where each sentence belongs by writing the correct answer choice letter in the chart. (**Note**: On the actual GED® test, you will click on each sentence and "drag" it into position in the chart.)

Benefits of the X1 in Space	Benefits of the X1 on Earth

   A. The X1 can measure, record, and stream back data to Mission Control.
   B. The X1 can assist wearers walking over varied terrain as well as on stairs.
   C. The X1 can provide paraplegics with physical support and motor function.
   D. The X1 can replicate crucial muscle-building exercises in microgravity.

4. What is the role of the details in paragraphs 5 and 6?

   A. They provide evidence that the X1 allows the wearer superhuman strength.
   B. They demonstrate the ways the X1 helps astronauts perform research.
   C. They illustrate different ways the X1 could be used in space and on Earth.
   D. They describe the X1's ability to allow greater freedom of movement.

---

[2] offloading: getting rid of

5. What can you infer about how the X1 would be used on Earth versus in space?

    A. On Earth: X1 would add weight to the wearer. In space: X1 would offload weight from the wearer.
    B. On Earth: X1 would provide vigorous physical activity. In space: X1 would promote relaxation.
    C. On Earth: X1 would provide wireless communication. In space: X1 would limit data streaming.
    D. On Earth: X1 would provide assistance. In space: X1 would provide resistance.

6. Fill in the blank with the word that expresses a neutral tone.

    The X1 has the potential to _____ the lives of people in space and on Earth.

    A. change
    B. supplement
    C. enrich
    D. refine

7. Based on the final paragraph of the passage, which of the following is a reasonable hypothesis?

    A. The X-1 will need government aid to succeed.
    B. The X-1 will benefit astronauts more than paraplegics.
    C. The X-1 will continue to improve with further research.
    D. The X-1 will inspire more scientists to study robotics.

8. What is the meaning of the word *impact* as it is used in paragraph 5?

    A. force
    B. duration
    C. effect
    D. collision

Use the passage to answer Questions 9–16.

Americans Use Many Types of Energy

1. Petroleum (oil) is the largest share of US primary energy consumption, followed by natural gas, coal, nuclear electric power, and renewable energy (including hydropower, wood, biofuels, biomass waste, wind, geothermal, and solar). Electricity is a secondary energy source that is generated from primary forms of energy.

2. The major energy users are residential and commercial buildings, industry, transportation, and electric power generators. The pattern of fuel use varies widely by sector. For example, petroleum oil provides 92% of the energy used for transportation, but only 1% of the energy used to generate electricity.

Domestic Energy Production versus Demand

3. In 2013, energy produced in the United States provided about 84% of the nation's energy needs. The remaining energy was supplied mainly by imports of petroleum.

4. The three major fossil fuels—petroleum, natural gas, and coal—accounted for most of the nation's energy production in 2013:

   - Natural gas—30%
   - Coal—24%
   - Petroleum (crude oil and natural gas plant liquids)—24%
   - Renewable energy—11%
   - Nuclear electric power—10%

The Mix of US Energy Production Changes

5. The three major fossil fuels—petroleum, natural gas, and coal—have dominated the US energy mix for more than 100 years. There have been several recent changes in US energy production. The share of coal produced from surface mines increased significantly from 25% in 1949 to 51% in 1971 to 66% in 2012. The remaining share was produced from underground mines. In 2013, natural gas production was higher than in any previous year. In recent years, more efficient and cost-effective drilling and production techniques have resulted in increased production of natural gas from shale formations.

6. Total US crude oil production generally decreased each year from a peak in 1970, but the trend reversed in 2010. In 2013, crude oil production was the highest since 1989. These increases were the result of increased use of horizontal drilling and hydraulic fracturing techniques, notably in North Dakota and Texas.

7   Natural gas plant liquids (NGPLs) are hydrocarbons that are separated as liquids from natural gas at processing plants. They are important ingredients for manufacturing plastics and gasoline. Propane is the only NGPL that is widely used for heating and cooking. Production of NGPL fluctuates with natural gas production, but the NGPL share of total US crude oil and petroleum field production increased from 8% in 1950 to 26% in 2013.

8   In 2013, total renewable energy production and consumption reached record highs of about 9 quadrillion Btu each. Hydroelectric power production in 2013 was about 9% below the 50-year average, but increases in biofuels' use and wind power generation increased the overall total contribution of renewable energy. Production of energy from wind and solar were at record highs in 2013.

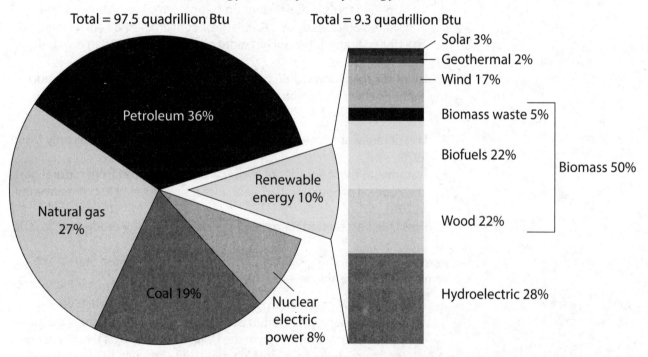

9. Which information is conveyed in both the text and the pie chart?

   A. Electricity is a secondary energy source generated by oil and gas.
   B. Fossil fuels account for most of US energy production.
   C. Renewable energy production reached a high point in 2013.
   D. Oil is the most-consumed energy source in the United States.

10. How does the data in the pie chart support the main idea in paragraph 1?

    A. The vertical bar in the chart represents renewable energy consumption.
    B. The same color in the chart represents both oil and coal consumption.
    C. The largest section in the chart represents petroleum consumption.
    D. The headings in the chart represent the total Btus of energy consumption.

Use the sentence below to answer Question 11:

In 2013, energy produced in the United States provided 84% of the nation's energy needs.

11. What inference can you make from this sentence?

    A. The United States is a country with few energy sources.
    B. The United States has discovered new forms of energy.
    C. The United States uses more energy than it can produce.
    D. The United States generates more energy than other nations.

12. Based on the passage, what conclusion can you draw about US energy consumption?

    A. The United States is committed to exploring renewable sources of oil.
    B. The United States is dependent on petroleum oil as an energy source.
    C. The United States is the world's largest consumer of oil and natural gas.
    D. The United States is producing more oil and electricity than ever before.

13. Which of the following would be the most relevant evidence to support the author's claim that trends in US energy production have changed in the past 50 years?

    A. Use of renewable sources of energy in the United States was only 5% in 1970.
    B. Natural gas plant liquids are hydrocarbons produced from natural gas.
    C. US crude oil production had been increasing since 1970 but decreased in 2010.
    D. Fossil fuels accounted for most of the nation's energy production in 2013.

14. Paragraphs 1–2 describe energy consumption in the United States. The remaining paragraphs develop the passage further by

    A. explaining how much energy the United States wastes each year.
    B. focusing on energy the United States obtains from foreign sources.
    C. discussing energy production in the United States and its recent changes.
    D. exploring new ways to generate renewable energy in the United States.

15. The underlying premise of paragraph 2 is that most energy consumption in the United States is due to

    A. residential use.
    B. manufacturing.
    C. transportation.
    D. technology.

16. What does paragraph 8 imply about energy production in the United States?

    A. Production of crude oil is stable.
    B. Production of renewable energy is rising.
    C. Production of hydroelectric power is outdated.
    D. Production of coal is unpopular.

Use the passage to answer Questions 17–24.

Relaxation Techniques

1   Relaxation is more than a state of mind; it physically changes the way your body functions. When your body is relaxed, breathing slows, blood pressure and oxygen consumption decrease, and some people report an increased sense of well-being. This is called the "relaxation response." Being able to produce the relaxation response by using relaxation techniques may counteract the effects of long-term stress, which may contribute to or worsen a range of health problems, including depression, digestive disorders, headaches, high blood pressure, and insomnia.

2   Relaxation techniques often combine breathing and focused attention to calm the mind and the body. Most methods require only brief instruction from a book or experienced practitioner before they can be done without assistance. These techniques may be most effective when practiced regularly and combined with good nutrition, regular exercise, and a strong social support system.

3   People may use relaxation techniques as part of a comprehensive plan to treat, prevent, or reduce symptoms of a variety of conditions, including stress, high blood pressure, chronic pain, insomnia, depression, labor pain, headache, cardiovascular disease, anxiety, chemotherapy side effects, and others.

4   According to the 2007 National Health Interview Survey, which included a comprehensive survey on the use of complementary health approaches by Americans, 12.7 percent of adults used deep-breathing exercises, 2.9 percent used progressive relaxation, and 2.2 percent used guided imagery, or focusing on pleasant images, for health purposes. Most of those people reported using a book to learn the techniques rather than seeing a practitioner.

5   To understand how consciously producing the relaxation response may affect your health, it is helpful to understand how your body responds to the opposite of relaxation—stress.

6   When you are under stress, your body releases hormones that produce the "fight-or-flight response." Heart rate and breathing rate go up, and then blood vessels narrow (restricting the flow of blood). This response allows energy to flow to parts of your body that need to take action, for example, the muscles and the heart. However useful this response may be in the short term, there is evidence that when your body remains in a stress state for a long time, emotional or physical damage can occur. Long-term or chronic stress (lasting months or years) may reduce your body's ability to fight off illness and lead to or worsen certain health conditions. Chronic stress may play a role in developing high blood pressure, headaches, and stomachache. Stress may worsen certain conditions, such as asthma. Stress has also been linked to depression, anxiety, and other mental illnesses.

7   In contrast to the stress response, the relaxation response slows the heart rate, lowers blood pressure, and decreases oxygen consumption and levels of stress hormones. Because relaxation is the opposite of stress, the theory is that voluntarily creating the relaxation response through regular use of relaxation techniques could counteract the negative effects of stress.

17. Another way to say *comprehensive*, as it is used in paragraph 3, is

    _____.

    A. useful
    B. known
    C. complete
    D. technical

18. Reread paragraph 6. Then place the steps in order by writing the correct phrase on each line to complete each sentence. (**Note**: On the actual GED® test, you will click on each answer choice and "drag" it into position in the chart.)

What Happens to Your Body Under Stress
First,
Then,
Next,
Finally,

    A. your heart rate and breathing rate go up.
    B. blood flows mostly to your muscles and heart.
    C. your blood vessels narrow to restrict flow.
    D. your body releases hormones.

19. The phrase "In contrast" in paragraph 7 helps emphasize the difference between

    A. blood pressure and heart rates.
    B. fight-or-flight responses.
    C. science and experimental medicine.
    D. stress and relaxation.

20. How does the structure of the passage support the author's main idea?

    A. The cause-and-effect structure allows the author to explain the negative effects of stress and the positive effects of relaxation techniques.
    B. The problem-solution structure allows the author to explain how readers can use relaxation techniques to offset the stress in their lives.
    C. The narrative structure allows the author to tell a story about his or her own experiences of using relaxation techniques to reduce stress.
    D. The pro-and-con structure allows the author to debate the types of relaxation techniques readers could use to deal with stress.

21. How does the author support the underlying assumption that most people prefer to live healthier, happier lives?

    A. by explaining step-by-step how to perform relaxation techniques
    B. by listing illnesses people may avoid through relaxation techniques
    C. by citing a survey that shows the benefits of relaxation techniques
    D. by quoting medical doctors about the benefits of relaxation techniques

Use the sentence below to answer Question 22:

When your body is relaxed, breathing slows, blood pressure and oxygen consumption decrease, and some people report an increased sense of well-being.

22. What inference can you make based on this sentence?

    A. Relaxation improves physical endurance.
    B. Relaxation promotes greater productivity.
    C. Relaxation benefits the mind and the body.
    D. Relaxation prevents the effects of disease.

Use the sentence below to answer Questions 23 and 24.

Because relaxation is the opposite of stress, the theory is that voluntarily creating the relaxation response through regular use of relaxation techniques could **counteract** the negative effects of stress.

23. In the following blank, write a word that is a synonym for the word *counteract* as it is used in the sentence: _____

24. In the following blank, write an antonym of the word *counteract* as it is used in the sentence: _____

Use the two passages to answer Questions 25–33. The first is an excerpt from a report on physical activity guidelines. The second is a fact sheet about physical activity.

Key Physical Activity Guidelines for Adults

1 . . . For substantial health benefits, adults should do at least 150 minutes (2 hours and 30 minutes) a week of moderate-intensity, or 75 minutes (1 hour and 15 minutes) a week of vigorous-intensity aerobic physical activity, or an equivalent combination of moderate- and vigorous-intensity aerobic activity. Aerobic activity should be performed in episodes of at least 10 minutes, and preferably, it should be spread throughout the week. . . .

2 Adults should also do muscle-strengthening activities that are moderate or high intensity and involve all major muscle groups on two or more days a week, as these activities provide additional health benefits. . . .

How Many Days a Week and for How Long?

3 Aerobic physical activity should preferably be spread throughout the week. Research studies consistently show that activity performed on at least three days a week produces health benefits. Spreading physical activity across at least three days a week may help reduce the risk of injury and avoid excessive fatigue.

4 Both moderate- and vigorous-intensity aerobic activity should be performed in episodes of at least 10 minutes. Episodes of this duration are known to improve cardiovascular fitness and some risk factors for heart disease and type 2 diabetes.

How Intense?

5 The Guidelines for adults focus on two levels of intensity: moderate-intensity activity and vigorous-intensity activity. To meet the Guidelines, adults can do either moderate-intensity or vigorous-intensity aerobic activities, or a combination of both. . . .

For More Information

6 . . . When using relative intensity, people pay attention to how physical activity affects their heart rate and breathing. As a rule of thumb, a person doing moderate-intensity aerobic activity can talk, but not sing, during the activity. A person doing vigorous-intensity activity cannot say more than a few words without pausing for a breath.

Different Aerobic Physical Activities and Intensities

7 There are numerous aerobic activities you can enjoy. What is most important is to understand the intensity of different kinds of aerobic

activities, so you may gain the necessary benefits from them. Some activities are moderate, which may be best for people beginning an exercise program for the first time or resuming exercise after a long absence to give the body time to adjust to the level of activity. Moderate-intensity activities include walking briskly (3 miles per hour or faster, but not race-walking), bicycling slower than 10 miles per hour, water aerobics, and general gardening.

8   More vigorous activities help you move from moderate exercise to a more challenging level of fitness or to maintain fitness once you have reached your desired health goal. These activities may include race-walking, jogging, or running; bicycling 10 miles an hour or faster; swimming laps; and heavy gardening, among others.

Be Active Your Way: A Fact Sheet for Adults

Why should I be physically active?

Physical activity can make you feel stronger and more alive. It is a fun way to be with your family or friends. It also helps you improve your health.

How many times a week should I be physically active?

It is up to you, but it is better to spread your activity throughout the week and to be active at least 3 days a week. . . .

How much physical activity do I need to do?

This chart tells you about the activities that are important for you to do. Do both aerobic activities and strengthening activities. Each offers important health benefits. And remember, some physical activity is better than none!

Aerobic Activities	If you choose activities at a **moderate** level, do at least **2 hours and 30 minutes** a week. If you choose vigorous activities, do at least **1 hour and 15 minutes** a week.	• Slowly build up the amount of time you do physical activities. The more time you spend, the more health benefits you gain. Aim for twice the amount of activity in the box at left. • Do at least 10 minutes at a time. • You can combine moderate and vigorous activities.
Muscle-Strengthening Activities	Do these at least **two days** a week.	Include all the major muscle groups such as legs, hips, back, chest, stomach, shoulders, and arms. Exercises for each muscle group should be repeated 8 to 12 times per session.

How can I tell an activity at a moderate level from a vigorous one?

Vigorous activities take more effort than moderate ones. Here are just a few moderate and vigorous aerobic physical activities. Do these for **10 minutes** or more at a time.

Moderate Activities

(I can talk while I do them, but I can't sing.)

- Ballroom and line dancing
- Biking on level ground or with few hills
- General gardening (raking, trimming shrubs)
- Tennis (doubles)
- Walking briskly
- Water aerobics

Vigorous Activities:

(I can only say a few words without stopping to catch my breath.)

- Aerobic dance and fast dancing
- Biking faster than 10 miles per hour
- Heavy gardening (digging, hoeing)
- Race-walking, jogging, or running
- Swimming fast or swimming laps
- Tennis (singles)

25. Which information does NOT appear in both the article and the fact sheet?

    A. lists of different moderate and vigorous activities
    B. advice on reducing the risk of injury and avoiding excessive fatigue
    C. explanations for why one should be physically active
    D. instructions for determining how intense an activity is

26. What is the purpose of the chart in the fact sheet showing levels of physical activity?

    A. It extends information about doing moderate versus vigorous activities.
    B. It clarifies the claim that aerobic activity improves one's health.
    C. It contradicts the idea that physical activity increases injuries.
    D. It emphasizes that some exercise is better than none.

27. How do the details in the last column of the fact sheet's chart help readers?

    A. They tell how to determine aerobic intensity.
    B. They list moderate and vigorous activities.
    C. They explain the benefits of physical activity.
    D. They provide instructions for how to exercise.

28. What is a key difference between the guidelines and the fact sheet?

    A. They are aimed at different audiences.
    B. They have different purposes.
    C. They use different writing styles.
    D. They emphasize different information.

29. What conclusion about American adults can you draw from the guidelines and the fact sheet?

    A. They work long hours and experience stress.
    B. They care a lot about improving their health.
    C. They are less active than teens and children.
    D. They do not get enough physical exercise.

30. Based on the details in the guidelines and the fact sheet, what generalization can you make?

    A. American children need more physical education classes in school.
    B. Americans benefit when they participate in regular physical exercise.
    C. American adults require a wide variety of enjoyable physical activities.
    D. American health agencies want to regulate citizens' physical fitness.

31. Which is a valid reason for adults to be physically active, according to both the guidelines and the fact sheet?

    A. Physical activity helps them bond with family and friends.
    B. Physical activity offers them an enjoyable way to waste time.
    C. Physical activity provides them with many health benefits.
    D. Physical activity makes them feel stronger and more alive.

32. Which word could be used in place of the word *vigorous* in the guidelines and the fact sheet?

    A. physical
    B. hearty
    C. exhausting
    D. persistent

33. What is the purpose of both the guidelines and the fact sheet? Write your answer on the following lines.

    _____

    _____

    _____

Questions 34–40 refer to the following excerpt from The Mound Builders *by George Bryce.*

1   A mound of the kind found in our region is a very much flattened cone, or round-topped hillock of earth. It is built usually, if not invariably where the soil is soft and easily dug, and it is generally possible to trace in its neighborhood the depression whence the mound material has been taken. The mounds are as a rule found in the midst of a fertile section of country, and it is pretty certain from this that the mound builders were agriculturists, and chose their dwelling places with their occupation in view, where the mounds are found. The mounds are found accordingly on the banks of the Rainy River and Red River, and their affluents in the Northwest, in other words upon our best land stretches, but not so far as observed around the Lake of the Woods, or in barren regions. Near fishing grounds they greatly abound. What seem to have been strategic points upon the river were selected for their sites. The promontory giving a view and so commanding a considerable stretch of river, the point at the junction of two rivers, or the debouchure of a river into a lake or vice versa is a favorite spot. At the Long Sault on Rainy River there are three or four mounds grouped together along a ridge. Here some persons of strong imagination profess to see remains of an ancient fortification, but to my mind this is mere fancy. Mounds in our region vary from 6 to 50 feet in height, and from 60 to 130 feet in diameter. Some are circular at the base, others are elliptical.

2   The mounds have long been known as occurring in Central America, in Mexico, and along the whole extent of the Mississippi valley from the Gulf of Mexico to the great lakes. Our Northwest has, however, been neglected in the accounts of the mound-bearing region. Along our Red River I can count some six or eight mounds that have been noted in late years, and from the banks having been peopled and cultivated I have little doubt that others have been obliterated. One formerly stood on the site of the new unfinished Canadian Pacific Hotel in this city. The larger number of those known are in the neighborhood of the rapids, 16 or 18 miles below Winnipeg where the fishing is good. In 1879 the Historical Society opened one of these, and obtained a considerable quantity of remains.

3   It is reported that there are mounds also on Nettley Creek, a tributary of the lower Red River, also on Lake Manitoba and some of its affluents. During the past summer it was my good fortune to visit the Rainy River, which lies some half way of the distance from Winnipeg to Lake Superior. In that delightful stretch of country, extending for 90 miles along the river there are no less than 21 mounds. These I identify with the mounds of Red River. The communication between Red and Rainy River is effected by ascending the Red Lake River, and coming by portage to a river running from the south into Rainy River. Both Red and Rainy River easily connect with the head waters of the Mississippi.

4   Our region then may be regarded as a self-contained district including the most northerly settlements of the strange race who built the mounds. I shall try to connect them with other branches of the same stock, lying further to the east and south. For convenience I shall speak of the extinct

people who inhabited our special region as the *Takawgamis,* or farthest north mound builders.

[*Source*: Project Gutenberg]

34. Which of the following is the best summary of the passage?

   A. The author describes mounds and the types of places they are located. He identifies various locations of mounds within his part of the country and attempts to categorize them.
   B. The author was out hiking when he discovered a native burial mound. This led him to explore other mounds in the region.
   C. A scientist excavates several burial mounds to learn more about the people who built them and how they lived.
   D. The author describes the ancient people who built mounds near his home. He then imagines what it must have been like for those people to travel from place to place.

35. Which of the following statements based on the passage is an opinion?

   A. Both Red River and Rainy River connect with the headwaters of the Mississippi.
   B. Rainy River lies about halfway between Winnipeg and Lake Superior.
   C. Our region, then, may be regarded as a self-contained district.
   D. At the Long Sault on Rainy River, there are three or four mounds grouped together along a ridge.

36. The author most likely lives in

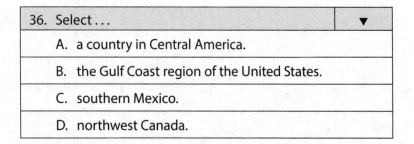

36. Select...	▼
A. a country in Central America.	
B. the Gulf Coast region of the United States.	
C. southern Mexico.	
D. northwest Canada.	

37. What does the author most likely mean when he says, "The communication between Red and Rainy River is effected by ascending the Red Lake River"?

   A. The way to get from the Red River to the Rainy River is to go up the Red Lake River.
   B. It is difficult to reach the Rainy River from the Red River.
   C. To talk to someone in the Red River area, one must first call someone in the Red Lake area.
   D. One cannot get from the Red River to the Rainy River over land.

38. Why does the author believe that the mound builders were farming people?

    A. Mounds are located near rivers.
    B. Excavated mounds reveal farm tools.
    C. People in those areas today are farmers.
    D. Mounds are found in fertile parts of the country.

39. Which of the following describes a mound?

    A. A square fortification
    B. A cone that is flat on top
    C. A broad pyramid
    D. A small clump of dirt

40. Which of the following best states the author's most likely purpose in writing this passage?

    A. The author seeks to educate readers about the mounds in his region because little has been published about them.
    B. The author argues that the mounds in his region were built by several different groups of people.
    C. The author wants readers to have instructions for how to build their own mounds.
    D. The author is trying to correct the misconception that the mounds were built by the *Takawgamis*.

CHAPTER 3
Argumentation and Persuasion

Use the passage to answer Questions 1–6.

The Value of Educating Girls

[Adapted from a blog posting by Carol Koppell, USAID Senior Coordinator for Gender Equality and Women's Empowerment]

1   When girls are educated, their families are healthier, they have fewer children, they wed later, and they have more opportunities to generate income. One extra year of primary school boosts a girl's future wages 10 to 20 percent, and an extra year of secondary school increases that earning potential by 15 to 25 percent. Education also helps moms take better care of their kids. According to the World Bank, each additional year of female education reduces child mortality by 18 per thousand births.

2   These are amazing statistics, but I've also been fortunate enough to see for myself the high returns of investing in education. While in Kabul, I met with an incredible group of young women who were educated entirely in post-Taliban Afghanistan. They reminded me how critically important education is to peace, prosperity, and empowerment.

3   Those young women represent the future for a country that had virtually no girls in school less than 15 years ago. Today, Afghan girls are more than a third of the students. I am proud that USAID is supporting community-based schools in Afghanistan and that our literacy effort is playing an instrumental role in ensuring that these girls get an education; it is an investment that will pay dividends for generations to come.

4   Globally, enormous progress has been made in closing the gender gap in primary education over the last 20 years. In most of the world today, a similar percentage of girls and boys attend primary schools, yet disparities endure—there are 3.6 million more girls out of school compared to boys around the world. Women still comprise the majority (two-thirds) of the illiterate. In sub-Saharan Africa and South Asia, obtaining an education remains particularly tough for women and girls. The World Bank estimates that half of the out-of-school girls in the world live in sub-Saharan Africa and one quarter of them live in South Asia.

5   It's not just about access. Compounding the problem is a lack of quality education. For example, in Malawi, a country in Southeast Africa, robust primary school enrollment and matriculation rates are reported. However, a closer inspection of the educational system reveals that many students finish their schooling without being able to read. Therefore, a focus on both the quality of education and enrollment rates is needed.

6   We know that educating women and girls has tremendous multiplying effects for families, communities, and societies. That is why USAID launched five leadership partnerships involving universities in the United States and in Armenia, Paraguay, Rwanda, and South Sudan to promote gender equality and women's leadership. These programs will promote and develop curricula and opportunities for women in business, agriculture, and education in order to increase women's access to higher education and advanced degrees, strengthen institutional capacity in research and education on women's leadership, and promote women's leadership through higher education extension and outreach to underserved communities.

7   We are very excited to be collaborating with academic institutions in the United States and abroad to advance women's leadership. These partnerships offer a meaningful and important opportunity to ensure women are empowered, ultimately advancing economies and societies globally.

1. What claim does the author make in paragraph 1 about the education of women and girls?

   A. It promotes peace and prosperity in war-torn regions.
   B. It fails to reduce worldwide illiteracy rates despite much funding.
   C. It leads to healthier, more productive lives for women and their families.
   D. It is the most urgent problem facing the world's developing nations today.

2. How does the author build her argument in paragraphs 1–4?

   A. by discussing the often poor quality of women's education worldwide
   B. by describing successes and ongoing challenges in women's education
   C. by focusing on women's education rates in sub-Saharan Africa and Asia
   D. by emphasizing USAID's role in creating women's educational partnerships

3. Which sentence contains evidence that supports the author's claim that it is important to educate women and girls?

   A. One extra year of primary school boosts a girl's future wage 10 to 20 percent, and an extra year of secondary school increases that earning potential by 15 to 25 percent.
   B. While in Kabul, I met with an incredible group of young women who were educated entirely in post-Taliban Afghanistan.
   C. In most of the world today, a similar percentage of girls and boys attend primary schools, yet disparities endure—there are 3.6 million more girls out of school compared to boys around the world.
   D. The World Bank estimates that half of the out-of-school girls in the world live in sub-Saharan Africa and one quarter of them live in South Asia.

4. The author's reasoning in paragraph 4 is supported because she

   A. presents personal observations about educated Afghan women.
   B. acknowledges the current educational disparities between girls and boys.
   C. cites an expert source of information about educational inequality.
   D. supports USAID's efforts to promote educational equality worldwide.

5. How does paragraph 5 contribute to the overall structure of the argument?

   A. It presents positive examples of women's education worldwide.
   B. It praises the high enrollment rates in Malawi primary schools.
   C. It inspires readers to support women's literacy programs.
   D. It emphasizes focusing on the quality of women's education.

6. What is the author's main point of view about the education of women and girls?

   A. It has failed because women "still comprise the majority (two-thirds) of the illiterate" around the world.
   B. It has created "tremendous multiplying effects for families, communities, and societies."
   C. It has been a worthwhile investment because she saw the results among "an incredible group of young women" in Afghanistan.
   D. It has had mixed results because many female "students finish their schooling without being able to read."

Use the following two passages to answer Questions 7–14.

Driverless Cars Are a Good Idea

1   Driverless cars are without a doubt safer and more convenient than the passenger cars driven today. Those who love innovation will love them. Those who don't crave new technology may still be won over by the cars' many positive features.

2   First, they are safer. These cars don't drink and drive; they can't fall asleep at the wheel; they won't text or experience road rage. The rates of traffic accidents and accident-related injury or death are sure to drop.

3   Second, their convenience is unmatched. Especially in cities, a major reason that people avoid driving—besides traffic—is to avoid the hassle of parking. When a driverless car reaches its destination, the passenger gets out, and the car parks itself. The owner simply summons it by smartphone when he or she needs it again. In addition, these cars will give people more free time. The hours now wasted sitting in a car during a long commute could be time spent in leisure activities such as reading, viewing a film, or even catching up on sleep.

4   Most important, studies show that driverless cars are cheaper and better for the environment. Car ownership will likely decline in favor of car-sharing systems, such as Zipcar. Anyone can use a driverless car. That means others—family members or friends—may use your driverless car when you are at work. This ability to share resources cuts down on the need to purchase multiple vehicles and will ultimately lead to fewer vehicles on the road. According to a study by MIT, driverless cars will reduce congestion and pollution, especially in cities, because fewer vehicles will be on the road.

5   This is not the first time cars would profoundly affect society. Henry Ford's Model-T made passenger cars available to the average person, a change that revolutionized transportation. Driverless cars are a new revolution that meshes with modern wants and needs in many significant ways.

Let's Reverse the Trend toward a Driverless Society

1   Driverless cars are an interesting concept, but they will not be good for people, the economy, or the environment. No one is really sure how driverless cars will act. While technological innovation is something we all want, driverless cars are machines still designed and made by humans; therefore, they will malfunction in unpredictable ways, just as regular cars do. The New Orleans Institute for Technological Studies notes that driverless cars are still in the experimental stage.

2   First, current tests reveal that a small percentage of driverless cars go off route, take wrong turns, or stop without warning. Riders will not have enough time to address these errors when they occur, especially if they are not paying

attention, and accidents will result. Pedestrians will have to be more cautious than ever with these unpredictable vehicles cruising the streets.

3   In a survey conducted by the Alliance of Automobile Manufacturers, 42% said that driverless cars were a bad idea. Only 33% said it was a good idea, and 24% of the 2,000 adults surveyed did not know whether cars that can pilot themselves were good or bad. Of those surveyed, 86% answered that the person "operating" a driverless car should still have a driver's license.

4   Finally, some say that driverless cars are energy savers, but the opposite is more likely. The ease of driving will result in people choosing individual cars over public transportation. People will not mind driving much longer distances if they can spend their time doing something they enjoy, and increased urban congestion and pollution will be the result.

5   The driverless car sounds like a good idea on the surface, but it does not truly benefit the American public. We should concentrate on building better vehicles for today's drivers, not fantasy vehicles that will create more problems than solutions.

7. Which sentence in the first essay contains evidence that supports the claim that driverless cars are good for the environment?

   A. These cars don't drink and drive; they can't fall asleep at the wheel; they won't text or experience road rage.
   B. The hours now wasted sitting in a car during a long commute could be time spent in leisure activities such as reading, viewing a film, or even catching up on sleep.
   C. According to a study by MIT, driverless cars will reduce congestion and pollution, especially in cities, because fewer vehicles will be on the road.
   D. Henry Ford's Model-T made passenger cars available to the average person, a change that revolutionized transportation, industry, and living space.

8. In the first essay, which sentence indicates that the writer is making a transition to a new idea?

   A. Anyone can use a driverless car.
   B. Those who love innovation will love them.
   C. This is not the first time cars would profoundly affect society.
   D. Second, their convenience is unmatched.

9. Both writers consider the impact of driverless cars on American society. How do their tones differ?

   A. The first writer is confident; the second writer is uncertain.
   B. The first writer is optimistic; the second writer is pessimistic.
   C. The first writer is critical; the second writer is open-minded.
   D. The first writer is neutral; the second writer is passionate.

10. Which of the following correctly states the writers' contrasting opinions about the driverless car?

    A. Writer 1: People will share the cars and reduce pollution.
       Writer 2: People will avoid public transportation and increase pollution.
    B. Writer 1: The cars will appeal to people who lack driving experience.
       Writer 2: The cars will most likely cause serious road accidents.
    C. Writer 1: Owners of driverless cars will become more productive.
       Writer 2: Owners of driverless cars will waste time on leisure activities.
    D. Writer 1: Driverless cars will change American life for the worse.
       Writer 2: Driverless cars will change American life for the better.

11. Which claim made by the second writer is not supported with valid evidence?

    A. Driverless cars will have unpredictable malfunctions.
    B. Driverless cars are bad for the economy.
    C. Driverless cars are disliked by most people.
    D. Driverless cars will reduce pollution.

Use this excerpt from the first passage to answer Question 12.

These cars don't drink and drive; they can't fall asleep at the wheel; they won't text or experience road rage. The rates of traffic accidents and accident-related injury or death are sure to drop.

12. What is the underlying premise in this paragraph?

    A. Human drivers should be banned from the roads.
    B. Texting and road rage contribute to car accidents.
    C. Computers are far less likely to make mistakes than humans.
    D. Driverless cars made by humans will still have accidents.

13. In which sentence from the second passage does the author acknowledge a different point of view from his or her own?

    A. In a survey conducted by the Alliance of Automobile Manufacturers, 42% said that driverless cars were a bad idea.
    B. No one is really sure how driverless cars will act.
    C. The ease of driving will result in people choosing individual cars over public transportation.
    D. Some say that driverless cars are energy savers, but the opposite is more likely.

14. What organizational structure do both writers use to present their arguments?

    A. chronological order
    B. point-by-point
    C. cause and effect
    D. problem-solution

Use the passage to answer Questions 15–22.

Adapted from the 1997 Inaugural Address by President William J. Clinton

1   The promise of America was born in the 18th century out of the bold conviction that we are all created equal. It was extended and preserved in the 19th century, when our Nation spread across the continent, saved the Union, and abolished the awful scourge of slavery.

2   Then, in turmoil and triumph, that promise exploded onto the world stage to make this the American Century. And what a century it has been. America became the world's mightiest industrial power, saved the world from tyranny in two World Wars and a long cold war, and time and again reached out across the globe to millions who, like us, longed for the blessings of liberty.

3   Along the way, Americans produced a great middle class and security in old age, built unrivaled centers of learning and opened public schools to all, split the atom and explored the heavens, invented the computer and the microchip, and deepened the wellspring of justice by making a revolution in civil rights for African-Americans and all minorities and extending the circle of citizenship, opportunity, and dignity to women.

4   Now, for the third time, a new century is upon us and another time to choose. We began the 19th century with a choice: to spread our Nation from coast to coast. We began the 20th century with a choice: to harness the industrial revolution to our values of free enterprise, conservation, and human decency. Those choices made all the difference. At the dawn of the 21st century, a free people must now choose to shape the forces of the information age and the global society, to unleash the limitless potential of all our people, and yes, to form a more perfect Union.

5   When last we gathered, our march to this new future seemed less certain than it does today. We vowed then to set a clear course to renew our Nation. In these four years, we have been touched by tragedy, exhilarated by challenge, strengthened by achievement. America stands alone as the world's indispensable nation. Once again, our economy is the strongest on Earth. Once again, we are building stronger families, thriving communities, better educational opportunities, a cleaner environment. Problems that once seemed destined to deepen, now bend to our efforts. Our streets are safer, and record numbers of our fellow citizens have moved from welfare to work. And once again, we have resolved for our time a great debate over the role of Government. Today we can declare: Government is not the problem, and Government is not the solution. We—the American people—we are the solution. Our Founders understood that well and gave us a democracy strong enough to endure for centuries, flexible enough to face our common challenges and advance our common dreams in each new day.

6   As times change, so Government must change. We need a new Government for a new century, humble enough not to try to solve all our problems for us but strong enough to give us the tools to solve our problems for ourselves, a Government that is smaller, lives within its means, and does more with less. Yet where it can stand up for our values and interests around the world, and where it can give Americans the power to make a real difference in their everyday lives, Government should do more, not less. The preeminent mission of our new Government is to give all Americans an opportunity, not a guarantee but a real opportunity, to build better lives.

7   Beyond that, my fellow citizens, the future is up to us. Our Founders taught us that the preservation of our liberty and our Union depends upon responsible citizenship. And we need a new sense of responsibility for a new century. There is work to do, work that Government alone cannot do: teaching children to read, hiring people off welfare rolls, coming out from behind locked doors and shuttered windows to help reclaim our streets from drugs and gangs and crime, taking time out of our own lives to serve others.

8   Each and every one of us, in our own way, must assume personal responsibility not only for ourselves and our families but for our neighbors and our Nation. Our greatest responsibility is to embrace a new spirit of community for a new century. For any one of us to succeed, we must succeed as one America. The challenge of our past remains the challenge of our future: Will we be one Nation, one people, with one common destiny, or not? Will we all come together, or come apart?

15. What is the relationship between paragraphs 1 and 2?

    A. Paragraph 1 discusses the causes of "the promise of America," and paragraph 2 explains its effects over several centuries.
    B. Paragraph 1 defines the concept of "the promise of America," and paragraph 2 extends the definition by providing examples.
    C. Paragraph 1 examines "the promise of America" during the 18th and 19th centuries, and paragraph 2 examines its development in the 20th century.
    D. Paragraph 1 explains what "the promise of America" is, and paragraph 2 distinguishes the promise from actual historical events.

16. President Clinton supports his claim that the United States is a nation of promise by including

    A. statements that qualify his initial ideas about "the promise of America."
    B. lists of actions that illustrate Americans' determination and success.
    C. anecdotes about hardworking US citizens and their communities.
    D. analogies that compare the United States to other great world civilizations.

17. After reading paragraph 5, what conclusion can you draw about the United States during President Clinton's term?

    A. The nation had lost power and prestige in the eyes of the world.
    B. The nation had been deeply tested by recent historical events.
    C. The nation had become stronger over the previous four years.
    D. The nation had experienced economic and political turmoil.

18. How does paragraph 6 contribute to the development of President Clinton's ideas?

    A. It introduces the president's concept of "the promise of America."
    B. It restates the president's claim about the challenges the nation faces.
    C. It describes events that happened during the president's first term.
    D. It outlines the president's view of what good government should do.

19. Which is the *best* summary of paragraph 4?

    A. The United States faces a new century, and its citizens must once again make difficult choices about the kind of nation they want it to be.
    B. Americans have achieved many accomplishments over three centuries, including establishing a technological revolution.
    C. The United States is a stronger nation than it was four years ago, and it will continue to thrive as it enters a new century.
    D. The purpose of a government is to provide its citizens with tools to solve problems at home and help other nations abroad.

20. When President Clinton uses the phrase "American Century" in paragraph 2, he suggests that

    A. the 1900s were a time in which Americans felt isolated as a nation.
    B. the United States was a powerful force in the world during the 1900s.
    C. the 1900s marked the end of American's influence in the world.
    D. the other nations of the world came under American rule during the 1900s.

21. Clinton uses the word *scourge* in paragraph 1 to

    A. emphasize the great suffering that slavery represented.
    B. stimulate his audience to keep them interested.
    C. prove that slavery is no longer an issue in America.
    D. impress listeners with his sophisticated vocabulary.

22. President Clinton's purpose for giving this speech is most likely

    A. to reassure Americans that his second term as president will be better than the first.
    B. to convince Americans to elect him for a second term as president.
    C. to inspire Americans as they move into his second term and a new century.
    D. to persuade Americans to allow changes to the government in his second term.

Use the passage to answer Questions 23–27.

from "The Whistle" by Benjamin Franklin

1 In my opinion we might all draw more good from it than we do, and suffer less evil, if we would take care not to give too much for *whistles*. For to me it seems that most of the unhappy people we meet with are become so by neglect of that caution.

2 When I was a child of seven years old, my friends, on a holiday, filled my pocket with coppers.[1] I went directly to a shop where they sold toys for children; and being charmed with the sound of a *whistle*, that I met by the way in the hands of another boy, I voluntarily offered and gave all my money for one. I then came home, and went whistling all over the house, much pleased with my *whistle*, but disturbing all the family. My brothers, and sisters, and cousins, understanding the bargain I had made, told me I had given four times as much for it as it was worth; put me in mind what good things I might have bought with the rest of the money; and laughed at me so much for my folly, that I cried with vexation; and the reflection gave me more chagrin than the *whistle* gave me pleasure.

3 This, however, was afterwards of use to me, the impression continuing on my mind; so that often, when I was tempted to buy some unnecessary thing, I said to myself, *Don't give too much for the whistle*; and I saved my money.

4 As I grew up, came into the world, and observed the actions of men, I thought I met with many, very many, *who gave too much for the whistle.*

5 When I saw one too ambitious of court favor, sacrificing his time in attendance on levees, his repose, his liberty, his virtue, and perhaps his friends, to attain it, I have said to myself, *This man gives too much for his whistle.*

6 When I saw another fond of popularity, constantly employing himself in political bustles, neglecting his own affairs, and ruining them by that neglect, *He pays, indeed*, said I, *too much for his whistle.*

7 If I knew a miser, who gave up every kind of comfortable living, all the pleasure of doing good to others, all the esteem of his fellow-citizens, and the joys of benevolent friendship, for the sake of accumulating wealth, *Poor man*, said I, *you pay too much for your whistle.*

8 When I met with a man of pleasure, sacrificing every laudable improvement of the mind, or of his fortune, to mere corporeal sensations, and ruining his health in their pursuit, *Mistaken man*, said I, *you are providing pain for yourself, instead of pleasure; you give too much for your whistle.*

9 If I see one fond of appearance, or fine clothes, fine houses, fine furniture, fine equipages, all above his fortune, for which he contracts debts, and ends his career in a prison, *Alas!* say I, *he has paid dear, very dear, for his whistle.*

---

[1] coppers: coins

10 When I see a beautiful sweet-tempered girl married to an ill-natured brute of a husband, *What a pity*, say I, *that she should pay so much for a whistle!*

11 In short, I conceive that great part of the miseries of mankind are brought upon them by the false estimates they have made of the value of things, and by their *giving too much for their whistles.*

23. In the passage, Franklin uses whistles as analogies for

    A. cherishing childhood memories.
    B. overvaluing useless things.
    C. setting long-term goals.
    D. wasting important opportunities.

24. What examples does Franklin use to support his claim that people should not "give too much for the whistle"? On the following lines, write two specific examples from the passage.

    _____
    _____
    _____
    _____
    _____

25. What is Franklin's primary purpose for writing "The Whistle"?

    A. to argue that people should be more thoughtful when making choices
    B. to suggest that people are confused because life offers too many choices
    C. to assert that schools should teach children to make better choices
    D. to contend that it is important to accept responsibility for your choices

26. How does the structure of paragraphs 2, 3, and 4 support Franklin's purpose?

    A. It outlines the step-by-step solution for wasting money on useless things.
    B. It explains the cause-and-effect relationship between greed and corruption.
    C. It narrates the lesson Franklin learned in childhood from overvaluing a toy.
    D. It compares the desire for material goods with the desire to do good.

Use the excerpt to answer Question 27.

In short, I conceive that great part of the miseries of mankind are brought upon them by the false estimates they have made of the value of things, and by their *giving too much for their whistles.*

27. What can you infer about Franklin's attitude toward his fellow human beings? He believes they

    A. are incapable of intelligent thought.
    B. waste their lives on unnecessary pursuits.
    C. will always be miserable creatures.
    D. deserve the consequences of bad choices.

Use this sentence to answer Questions 28–30.

My brothers, and sisters, and cousins, understanding the bargain I had made, told me I had given four times as much for it as it was worth; put me in mind what good things I might have bought with the rest of the money; and laughed at me so much for my folly, that I cried with **vexation**; and the **reflection** gave me more **chagrin** than the *whistle* gave me pleasure.

28. In the blank, write a word that is a synonym for the word *vexation,* as it is used in the sentence: _____.

29. In the blank, write a synonym for the word *reflection* as it is used in the sentence: _____.

30. In the blank, write the bolded word that is neutral, with no negative connotation: _____.

Use the following two passages to answer Questions 31–42.

Adapted from President Gerald Ford's Address on Energy Policy (May 27, 1975)

1   Here are the facts and figures that will not go away. The United States is dependent on foreign sources for about 37 percent of its present petroleum needs. In 10 years, if we do nothing, we will be importing more than half our oil at prices fixed by others—if they choose to sell to us at all. In 2½ years, we will be twice as vulnerable to a foreign oil embargo as we were two winters ago.

2   We are now paying out $25 billion a year for foreign oil. Five years ago we paid out only $3 billion annually. Five years from now, if we do nothing, who knows how many more billions will be flowing out of the United States. These are not just American dollars, these are American jobs.

3   The Congress has concentrated its attention on conservation measures such as a higher gasoline tax. The Congress has done little or nothing to stimulate production of new energy sources here at home. At Elk Hills Naval Petroleum Reserve in California, I saw oil wells waiting to produce 300,000 barrels a day if the Congress would change the law to permit it.

4   There are untold millions of barrels more in our Alaskan petroleum reserves and under the Continental Shelf.[2] We could save 300,000 barrels a day if only the Congress would allow more electric power plants to substitute American coal for foreign oil. Peaceful atomic power, which we pioneered, is advancing faster abroad than at home.

5   Still the Congress does nothing about energy. We are today worse off than we were in January. Domestic oil production is going down, down, down. Natural gas production is starting to dwindle. And many areas face severe shortages next winter. Coal production is still at the levels of the 1940s. Foreign oil suppliers are considering another price increase. I could go on and on, but you know the facts. This country needs to regain its independence from foreign sources of energy, and the sooner the better.

6   There is no visible energy shortage now, but we could have one overnight. We do not have an energy crisis, but we may have one next winter. We do have an energy problem, a very grave problem, but one we can still manage and solve if we are successful internationally and can act decisively domestically....

7   First, I will impose an additional $1 import fee on foreign crude oil and 60 cents on refined products, effective June 1. I gave the Congress its 60 days plus an extra 30 days to do something—but nothing has been done since January. Higher fees will further discourage the consumption of imported fuel and may generate some constructive action when the Congress comes back.

---

[2] Continental Shelf: the edge of a continent that lies beneath the ocean

8   Second, as I directed on April 30, the Federal Energy Administration has completed public hearings on decontrol[3] of old domestic oil. I will submit a decontrol plan to Congress shortly after it reconvenes. Along with it, I will urge the Congress to pass a windfall profits tax[4] with a plowback provision.

9   These two measures would prevent unfair gains by oil companies from decontrol prices, furnish a substantial incentive to increase domestic energy production, and encourage conservation.

10 When I talk about energy, I am talking about jobs. Our American economy runs on energy—no energy, no jobs. In the long run, it is just that simple.

Adapted from the Response to the State of the Union Address of President Gerald Ford by the Honorable Morris K. Udall (January 23, 1975)

1   The foremost fact we must face is that the absolute prerequisite to economic recovery is substantial and immediate energy conservation. We import nearly 40 percent of our oil, and the proportion, as well as the absolute quantity, is still increasing. The President's stated goal—reducing oil consumption by 1 million barrels a day this year—is simply inadequate, representing only 5 percent of our oil consumption and just 3 percent of our overall energy demand. The harsh fact is that we must double this cut . . . if we are serious about moving toward stability.

2   . . . The President has chosen a clumsy, unjust, and economically disastrous route. He would force energy prices sky high, then have the Government turn its back on the problem and let the forces of the marketplace cut energy use across the board . . .

3   Let me detail what this means to each American—what the picture would look like if Congress enacted all the President's proposals:

- The price of gasoline would rise at least 10 cents a gallon. That is an increase of 20 percent;
- The price of electricity would rise by at least 15 percent;
- The price of home heating oil would go up 20 to 25 percent, depending on the region;
- The price of decontrolled domestic crude oil would more than double, rising from the present $5.25 a barrel to the $10 uncontrolled level . . . ;
- The price of decontrolled interstate natural gas will soar to many times the current level—no one can predict exactly how high. . . .

4   The President's program would raise the Nation's energy bill by $40 to $50 billion annually. His tax package—including the inadequate windfall profits tax—would recapture only $30 billion of that, with the rest—up to $20 billion—remaining in the hands of the energy suppliers. . . .

---

[3] decontrol: remove control of something; repeal a law
[4] windfalls profit tax: tax placed on an unexpectedly large profit, often one gained unfairly

5   I recognize, as does the President, that ending energy waste is not enough. We must expand our domestic energy sources to meet the inevitable rise in demand that will come with the end of the recession. But where the President's conservation goals are too modest, his production goals are excessive and unrealistic. He ignores land shortages and siting problems, severe water shortages in the West, the overwhelming environmental problems associated with oil shale development and the many serious problems which must be solved before nuclear energy can be depended upon. Above all, the President ignores the enormous burdens such development would place on our already overstrained capital market.

6   I believe that the President and Congress must put the emphasis on cutting the rate of growth of energy use, rather than climbing back onto the old treadmill, trying to satisfy an unrestrained appetite for cheap energy. Nearly a year ago I introduced legislation to make an explicit commitment to cutting the rate of growth from nearly 5 to 2 percent per year. Since then, two major studies . . . have concluded that such a limited rate of energy growth can be achieved without economic harm. It is time to stop deluding ourselves, to stop thinking we can bring back the good old days of cheap and abundant energy.

7   They are gone—at least for a generation—perhaps forever—and we must adjust our habits accordingly.

Use the first passage to answer Questions 31–34:

31. What inference can you make about Congress based on paragraphs 3 and 4?

    A. It has refused to take responsibility for the current energy problem.
    B. It has worsened the energy problem by refusing to enact new laws.
    C. It has focused only on the environmental impact of the energy problem.
    D. It has devoted time to the energy problem at the expense of other issues.

32. Which sentence supports Ford's claim that America has "an energy problem"?

    A. There are untold millions of barrels more in our Alaskan petroleum reserves and under the Continental Shelf.
    B. Peaceful atomic power, which we pioneered, is advancing faster abroad than at home.
    C. The United States is dependent on foreign sources for about 37 percent of its present petroleum needs.
    D. Five years from now, if we do nothing, who knows how many more billions will be flowing out of the United States.

33. What is the relationship of paragraph 9 to paragraphs 7–8?

    A. It explains the effects of the actions described in paragraphs 7–8.
    B. It provides a solution to the problems noted in paragraphs 7–8.
    C. It establishes evidence to support the plan detailed in paragraphs 7–8.
    D. It warns of the consequences of the process outlined in paragraphs 7–8.

Use the following excerpt to answer Question 34:

There are untold millions of barrels more in our Alaskan petroleum reserves and under the Continental Shelf. We could save 300,000 barrels a day if only the Congress would allow more electric power plants to substitute American coal for foreign oil. Peaceful atomic power, which we pioneered, is advancing faster abroad than at home.

34. Identify Ford's implicit and explicit purposes for including this paragraph in his speech by writing each answer choice letter in the appropriate column. (**Note**: On the actual GED® test, you will click on each choice and "drag" it into position in the chart.)

Explicit Purpose	Implicit Purpose

A. to blame Congress for its lack of effective response to the energy problem
B. to suggest that the United States fails to compete regarding the use of atomic power
C. to introduce measures for developing forms of renewable energy sources
D. to emphasize that Americans have been consuming too much fossil fuel

35. What opposing claims do Ford and Udall make about the benefits of fees on imported fuel?

A. Ford says they will inspire Congress to increase domestic oil production; Udall says they will make the United States more oil dependent.
B. Ford says they will reduce US consumption of foreign oil; Udall says they will increase the nation's energy costs.
C. Ford says they will encourage Americans to conserve energy; Udall says they will cause another recession.
D. Ford says they will create more American jobs; Udall says they will result in huge profits for energy suppliers.

36. How does Udall build his argument against Ford's plan for addressing the energy crisis?

    A. He cites a survey about the impact of reduced energy use.
    B. He attacks Ford personally as being "clumsy" and "unjust."
    C. He quotes statistics about how much oil the United States imports.
    D. He lists drawbacks about oil production that Ford ignores.

37. Which of Ford's claims is not supported by valid, concrete evidence?

    A. Production of natural gas is decreasing.
    B. Congress is slow to pass energy laws.
    C. The energy crisis is costing American jobs.
    D. The amount of oil reserves is limited.

38. What technique do Ford's and Udall's speeches share?

    A. Both use statistics to shame Congress into action.
    B. Both use factual evidence to establish an urgent tone.
    C. Both use emotional appeals to move listeners to change.
    D. Both use an informal style to communicate serious ideas.

39. What is Ford's attitude toward increased energy production?

    A. It will lessen dependence on foreign fuel.
    B. It will result in a loss of jobs.
    C. It will occur only if Congress enacts new laws.
    D. It will cause the price of gasoline to stabilize.

40. Unlike Ford, Udall believes increased energy production will

    A. create environmental problems for America.
    B. help the American economy recover.
    C. increase America's hunger for cheap fuel.
    D. lower Americans' annual heating costs.

41. In paragraph 5, Udall distinguishes his position from Ford's by stating that

    A. Ford's goal to increase production is too unrealistic.
    B. Ford's goal to end energy waste is too expensive.
    C. Ford's goal to conserve energy is too complicated.
    D. Ford's goals for creating jobs are too ambitious.

Use the excerpt below to answer Question 42:

Still the Congress does nothing about energy. We are today worse off than we were in January. Domestic oil production is going down, down, down. Natural gas production is starting to dwindle.

42. How does Ford use language in this excerpt to reinforce his ideas about oil production?

   A. He makes an analogy.
   B. He repeats a key word.
   C. He creates a compelling rhythm.
   D. He uses parallel construction.

CHAPTER 4
Literature

Use the passage to answer Questions 1–5.

Adapted from *Pride and Prejudice* by Jane Austen

1   Mr. Bingley was good-looking and gentlemanlike . . . and easy, unaffected manners. His sisters were fine women, with an air of decided fashion. His brother-in-law, Mr. Hurst, merely looked the gentleman; but his friend Mr. Darcy soon drew the attention of the room by his fine, tall person, handsome features, noble mien,[1] and the report which was in general circulation within five minutes after his entrance, of his having ten thousand a year.[2] The gentlemen pronounced him to be a fine figure of a man, the ladies declared he was much handsomer than Mr. Bingley, and he was looked at with great admiration for about half the evening, till his manners gave a disgust which turned the tide of his popularity; for he was discovered to be proud; to be above his company, and above being pleased. . . .

2   Mr. Bingley had soon made himself acquainted with all the principal people in the room; he was lively and unreserved, danced every dance, was angry that the ball closed so early, and talked of giving one himself at Netherfield. Such amiable qualities must speak for themselves. What a contrast between him and his friend! Mr. Darcy danced only once with Mrs. Hurst and once with Miss Bingley, declined being introduced to any other lady, and spent the rest of the evening in walking about the room, speaking occasionally to one of his own party.[3] His character was decided. He was the proudest, most disagreeable man in the world, and everybody hoped that he would never come there again. Amongst the most violent against him was Mrs. Bennet, whose dislike of his general behaviour was sharpened into particular resentment by his having slighted one of her daughters.

3   Elizabeth Bennet had been obliged, by the scarcity of gentlemen, to sit down for two dances; and during part of that time, Mr. Darcy had been standing near enough for her to hear a conversation between him and Mr. Bingley, who came from the dance for a few minutes, to press his friend to join it.

4   "Come, Darcy," said he, "I must have you dance. I hate to see you standing about by yourself in this stupid manner. You had much better dance."

---

[1] mien: manner or appearance
[2] ". . . his having ten thousand a year": This means Darcy is wealthy. At the time the passage was written, his fortune would have been the equivalent of over half a million dollars.
[3] "his own party": the friends and family who came with Darcy to the party

5   "I certainly shall not. You know how I detest it, unless I am particularly acquainted with my partner. At such an assembly as this it would be insupportable. Your sisters are engaged, and there is not another woman in the room whom it would not be a punishment to me to stand up with."

6   "I would not be so fastidious as you are," cried Mr. Bingley, "for a kingdom! Upon my honor, I never met with so many pleasant girls in my life as I have this evening; and there are several of them you see uncommonly pretty."

7   "*You* are dancing with the only handsome girl in the room," said Mr. Darcy, looking at the eldest Miss Bennet.

8   "Oh! She is the most beautiful creature I ever beheld! But there is one of her sisters sitting down just behind you, who is very pretty, and I dare say very agreeable. Do let me ask my partner to introduce you."

9   "Which do you mean?" and turning round he looked for a moment at Elizabeth [Bennet], till catching her eye, he withdrew his own and coldly said: "She is tolerable, but not handsome enough to tempt *me*; I am in no humor at present to give consequence to young ladies who are slighted by other men. You had better return to your partner and enjoy her smiles, for you are wasting your time with me."

10   Mr. Bingley followed his advice. Mr. Darcy walked off; and Elizabeth remained with no very cordial feelings toward him. She told the story, however, with great spirit among her friends; for she had a lively, playful disposition, which delighted in anything ridiculous.

1. What event in the passage causes a conflict?

    A. Darcy's refusal to dance with ladies outside his party
    B. Darcy's talk of hosting a dance at Netherfield
    C. Darcy's dance with the elder Miss Bennet
    D. Darcy's boast of his exceptional dance skills

Use the following excerpt to answer Question 2:

Mr. Darcy walked off; and Elizabeth remained with no very cordial feelings toward him. She told the story, however, with great spirit among her friends; for she had a lively, playful disposition, which delighted in anything ridiculous.

2. What can you infer about the character of Elizabeth?

    A. She has a carefree manner and is rarely upset.
    B. She has a great wit and can be scornful.
    C. She is oversensitive and feels deeply offended.
    D. She is a serious intellectual and dislikes parties.

3. _____ is another word with the same meaning as *slighted*, as it is used in paragraph 2.

    A. charmed
    B. reduced
    C. ignored
    D. confused

4. Place the following events in the order that they happen in the story. Write the letter of each sentence in the appropriate box. (**Note**: On the actual GED® test, you will click on each sentence and "drag" it into position in the chart.)

    Order of Events

1.
2.
3.
4.

    A. The crowd admires Mr. Darcy's appearance and fortune.
    B. Mr. Bingley encourages Mr. Darcy to dance with the ladies.
    C. Elizabeth Bennet tells friends about Mr. Darcy's behavior.
    D. Mr. Darcy offends Mrs. Bennet by slighting her daughter.

5. What can you infer about Mr. Bingley and Mr. Darcy's relationship?

    A. They are companions, but Bingley tends to compete with Darcy.
    B. They are neighbors, but Darcy's wealth separates them socially.
    C. They are friends, but Bingley has little influence over Darcy.
    D. They are acquaintances, but Darcy rarely visits Bingley's home.

Use this passage to answer Questions 6–10.

Adapted from "The Diamond as Big as the Ritz" by F. Scott Fitzgerald

1   John's first two years there[4] passed pleasantly. The fathers of all the boys were money-kings, and John spent his summer visiting at fashionable resorts. While he was very fond of all the boys he visited, their fathers struck him as being much of a piece,[5] and in his boyish way he often wondered at their exceeding sameness. When he told them where his home was they would ask jovially, "Pretty hot down there?" and John would muster a faint smile and answer, "It certainly is."[6] His response would have been heartier had they not all made this joke—at best varying it with, "Is it hot enough for you down there?" which he hated just as much.

2   In the middle of his second year at school, a quiet, handsome boy named Percy Washington had been put in John's form. The newcomer was pleasant in his manner and exceedingly well dressed even for St. Midas's, but for some reason he kept aloof from the other boys. The only person with whom he was intimate was John T. Unger, but even to John he was entirely uncommunicative concerning his home or his family. That he was wealthy went without saying, but beyond a few such deductions John knew little of his friend . . . when Percy invited him to spend the summer at his home "in the West" [h]e accepted, without hesitation.

3   It was only when they were in the train that Percy became, for the first time, rather communicative. One day while they were eating lunch in the dining-car and discussing the imperfect characters of several of the boys at school, Percy suddenly changed his tone and made an abrupt remark.

4   "My father," he said, "is by far the richest man in the world."

5   "Oh," said John politely. He could think of no answer to make to this confidence. He considered "That's very nice," but it sounded hollow and was on the point of saying, "Really?" but refrained since it would seem to question Percy's statement. And such an astounding statement could scarcely be questioned.

6   "By far the richest," repeated Percy.

7   "I was reading in the *World Almanac*," began John, "that there was one man in America with an income of over five million a year and four men with incomes of over three million a year, and—"

8   "Oh, they're nothing." Percy's mouth was a half-moon of scorn. "Catch-penny capitalists, financial small-fry, petty merchants and money-lenders. My father could buy them out and not know he'd done it."

---

[4] at a private boarding school in the Northeast
[5] being much of a piece: being predictable
[6] John comes from Hades, a small town on the Mississippi River. *Hades* is also a modern-day synonym for *hell*.

9 "But how does he—"

10 "Why haven't they put down *his* income-tax? Because he doesn't pay any. At least he pays a little one—but he doesn't pay any on his *real* income."

11 "He must be very rich," said John simply. "I'm glad. I like very rich people. The richer a fella is, the better I like him."

12 There was a look of passionate frankness upon his dark face. "I visited the Schnlitzer-Murphys last Easter. Vivian Schnlitzer-Murphy had rubies as big as hen's eggs, and sapphires that were like globes with lights inside them—"

13 "I love jewels," agreed Percy enthusiastically. "Of course I wouldn't want any one at school to know about it, but I've got quite a collection myself. I used to collect them instead of stamps."

14 "And diamonds," continued John eagerly. "The Schnlitzer-Murphys had diamonds as big as walnuts—"

15 "That's nothing." Percy had leaned forward and dropped his voice to a low whisper. "That's nothing at all. My father has a diamond bigger than the Ritz-Carlton Hotel."

6. Based on the details in paragraph 1, what can you infer about John?

    A. He cares deeply about how people perceive him.
    B. He shares the values of the wealthy men he meets.
    C. He attends fashionable, high society parties regularly.
    D. He speaks politely but thinks critically of others.

7. How do paragraphs 3 and 4 contribute to the development of the story?

    A. They establish the fact that John and Percy's friendship is fake.
    B. They signal the shift when Percy begins to speak freely to John.
    C. They mark the point at which John recognizes he is inferior to Percy.
    D. They give background details about Percy's and John's childhoods.

8. What inference can you make about John based on his reaction to Percy's declaration in paragraph 4?

    A. John feels pleased that Percy confides in him.
    B. John disapproves of Percy's boasting.
    C. John questions Percy while trying to avoid offense.
    D. John believes Percy is lying but is too polite to say so.

Use the following excerpt to answer Question 9:

"And diamonds," continued John eagerly. "The Schnlitzer-Murphys had diamonds as big as walnuts—"

9. Why does John use the phrase "diamonds as big as walnuts"?

    A. to convey the exact size of the jewels to Percy
    B. to make Percy laugh with a humorous remark
    C. to engage in meaningless conversation with Percy
    D. to impress Percy with his acquaintances' wealth

10. What conclusion can you draw about John and Percy's friendship?

    A. It has the capacity to endure throughout the boys' lives.
    B. It is based on the boys' similar interests and tastes.
    C. It provides both boys with needed emotional support.
    D. It challenges the boys to rethink their ideas about wealth.

Use the passage to answer Questions 11–15.

Adapted from *The Secret Garden* by Frances Hodges Burnett

1. Many things happened during the hours in which she slept so heavily, but she was not disturbed by the wails and the sound of things being carried in and out of the bungalow.[7]

2. When she awakened she lay and stared at the wall. The house was perfectly still. She had never known it to be so silent before. She heard neither voices nor footsteps, and wondered if everybody had got well of the cholera and all the trouble was over. She wondered also who would take care of her now her Ayah was dead. There would be a new Ayah, and perhaps she would know some new stories. Mary had been rather tired of the old ones. She did not cry because her nurse had died. She was not an affectionate child and had never cared much for any one. The noise and hurrying about and wailing over the cholera[8] had frightened her, and she had been angry because no one seemed to remember that she was alive. Everyone was too panic-stricken to think of a little girl no one was fond of. When people had the cholera it seemed that they remembered nothing but themselves. But if everyone had got well again, surely someone would remember and come to look for her.

3. But no one came, and as she lay waiting the house seemed to grow more and more silent. She heard something rustling on the matting and when she looked down she saw a little snake gliding along and watching her with eyes like jewels. She was not frightened, because he was a harmless little thing who would not hurt her and he seemed in a hurry to get out of the room. He slipped under the door as she watched him.

4. "How queer and quiet it is," she said. "It sounds as if there was no one in the bungalow but me and the snake."

5. Almost the next minute she heard footsteps . . . They were men's footsteps, and the men entered the bungalow and talked in low voices. No one went to meet or speak to them and they seemed to open doors and look into rooms.

6. "What desolation!" she heard one voice say. "That pretty, pretty woman! I suppose the child, too. I heard there was a child, though no one ever saw her."

7. Mary was standing in the middle of the nursery when they opened the door a few minutes later. She looked an ugly, cross little thing and was frowning because she was beginning to be hungry and feel disgracefully neglected. The first man who came in was an officer she had once seen talking to her father. He looked tired and troubled, but when he saw her he was so startled that he almost jumped back.

---

[7] bungalow: small, one-story house
[8] cholera: often fatal infectious disease

8   "Barney!" he cried out. "There is a child here! A child alone! In a place like this! Mercy on us, who is she!"

9   "I am Mary Lennox," the little girl said, drawing herself up stiffly. She thought the man was very rude to call her father's bungalow "A place like this!" "I fell asleep when everyone had the cholera and I have only just wakened up. Why does nobody come?"

10 "It is the child no one ever saw!" exclaimed the man, turning to his companions. "She has actually been forgotten!"

11 "Why was I forgotten?" Mary said, stamping her foot. "Why does nobody come?"

12 The young man whose name was Barney looked at her sadly. Mary even thought she saw him wink his eyes as if to wink tears away.

13 "Poor little kid!" he said. "There is nobody left to come."

11. Based on the details in paragraph 2, what can you infer about Mary?

    A. She is a beautiful child who has loving parents.
    B. She is a lonely child who possesses a vivid imagination.
    C. She is an unpleasant child who is not well liked by others.
    D. She is an intelligent child who understands her situation.

12. Which incident leads up to the events described in the passage?

    A. A war forces soldiers to seek shelter in Mary's house.
    B. A disease kills the adults caring for young Mary.
    C. A natural disaster separates Mary from her parents.
    D. A snake has bitten Mary's nurse by surprise.

Use the following excerpt to answer Question 13:

The young man whose name was Barney looked at her sadly. Mary even thought she saw him wink his eyes as if to wink tears away.

13. Barney's "wink" shows that he feels

    A. arrogant.
    B. sympathetic.
    C. depressed.
    D. brave.

14. How are Mary and the snake alike?

    A. Both are fending for themselves.
    B. Both are recovering from the cholera.
    C. Both are afraid of what might happen.
    D. Both are trapped in the empty house.

Use the following excerpt to answer Question 15:

"I am Mary Lennox," the little girl said, drawing herself up stiffly.

15. Which word would change the tone and meaning of the sentence if it replaced *stiffly*?

    A. rigidly
    B. proudly
    C. grandly
    D. gently

Use the passage to answer Questions 16–20.

Adapted from "To Build a Fire" by Jack London

1   The man flung a look back along the way he had come. The Yukon[9] lay a mile wide and hidden under three feet of ice. On top of this ice were as many feet of snow. It was all pure white, rolling in gentle undulations where the ice-jams of the freeze-up had formed. North and south, as far as his eye could see, it was unbroken white, save for a dark hair-line that curved and twisted from around the spruce-covered island to the south, and that curved and twisted away into the north, where it disappeared behind another spruce-covered island. This dark hair-line was the trail—the main trail. . . .

2   But all this—the mysterious, far-reaching hair-line trail, the absence of sun from the sky, the tremendous cold, and the strangeness and weirdness of it all—made no impression on the man. It was not because he was long used to it. He was a new-comer in the land . . . and this was his first winter. The trouble with him was that he was without imagination. He was quick and alert in the things of life, but only in the things, and not in the significances. Fifty degrees below zero meant eighty odd degrees of frost. Such fact impressed him as being cold and uncomfortable, and that was all. It did not lead him to meditate upon his frailty as a creature of temperature, and upon man's frailty in general, able only to live within certain narrow limits of heat and cold; and from there on it did not lead him to the conjectural field of[10] immortality and man's place in the universe. Fifty degrees below zero stood for a bite of frost that hurt and that must be guarded against by the use of mittens, ear-flaps, warm moccasins, and thick socks. Fifty degrees below zero was to him just precisely fifty degrees below zero. That there should be anything more to it than that was a thought that never entered his head.

3   As he turned to go on, he spat speculatively. There was a sharp, explosive crackle that startled him. He spat again. And again, in the air, before it could fall to the snow, the spittle crackled. He knew that at fifty below spittle crackled on the snow, but this spittle had crackled in the air. Undoubtedly it was colder than fifty below—how much colder he did not know. But the temperature did not matter. He was bound for the old claim[11] on the left fork of Henderson Creek, where the boys were already. . . . He would be in to camp by six o'clock; a bit after dark, it was true, but the boys would be there, a fire would be going, and a hot supper would be ready. As for lunch, he pressed his hand against the protruding bundle under his jacket. It was also under his shirt, wrapped up in a handkerchief and lying against the naked skin. It was the only way to keep the biscuits from freezing. He smiled agreeably to himself as he thought of those biscuits, each

---

[9] The Yukon: a land area in northwest Canada bordering the Arctic Ocean
[10] the conjectural field of: consider the possibility of
[11] claim: a piece of land of which someone has declared ownership

cut open and sopped in bacon grease, and each enclosing a generous slice of fried bacon.

4   . . . He was surprised, however, at the cold. It certainly was cold, he concluded, as he rubbed his numbed nose and cheek-bones with his mittened hand. He was a warm-whiskered man, but the hair on his face did not protect the high cheek-bones and the eager nose that thrust itself aggressively into the frosty air.

5   At the man's heels trotted a dog, a big native husky, the proper wolf-dog, grey-coated and without any visible or temperamental difference from its brother, the wild wolf. The animal was depressed by the tremendous cold. It knew that it was no time for travelling. Its instinct told it a truer tale than was told to the man by the man's judgment. In reality, it was not merely colder than fifty below zero; it was colder than sixty below, than seventy below. It was seventy-five below zero. Since the freezing-point is thirty-two above zero, it meant that one hundred and seven degrees of frost obtained. The dog did not know anything about thermometers. Possibly in its brain there was no sharp consciousness of a condition of very cold such as was in the man's brain. But the brute had its instinct. It experienced a vague but menacing apprehension that subdued it and made it slink along at the man's heels, and that made it question eagerly every unwonted movement of the man as if expecting him to go into camp or to seek shelter somewhere and build a fire. The dog had learned fire, and it wanted fire, or else to burrow under the snow and cuddle its warmth away from the air.

16. Write the letter of the phrase that describes either the man or the dog in the appropriate column. (**Note**: On the actual GED® test, you will click on each word and "drag" it into position in the chart.)

Man	Dog

   A. observes others' actions
   B. lacks a sense of imagination
   C. ignores obvious dangers
   D. lives primarily by instinct
   E. recognizes dangers
   F. feels in control

17. In paragraph 3, the detail about the frozen spittle helps readers infer that the setting is

   A. rough.
   B. bleak.
   C. changing.
   D. remote.

18. What effect does the temperature have on the man in the first two paragraphs?

    A. It surprises him with its intensity.
    B. It forces him to turn back.
    C. It prompts him to change plans.
    D. It makes little impression on him.

Use the following excerpt to answer Question 19:

It did not lead him to meditate upon his frailty as a creature of temperature, and upon man's frailty in general, able only to live within certain narrow limits of heat and cold . . .

19. Which word has the opposite connotation of *frailty*, as it is used in the sentence?

    A. distrust
    B. potential
    C. strength
    D. fault

20. What contrast do the man and the dog represent?

    A. The man represents imagination; the dog represents reason.
    B. The man represents ignorance; the dog represents disloyalty.
    C. The man represents judgment; the dog represents instinct.
    D. The man represents freedom; the dog represents law.

Use the passage to answer Questions 21–25.

Adapted from "The Kiss" by Kate Chopin

1. . . . They were talking low, of indifferent things which plainly were not the things that occupied their thoughts. She knew that [Brantain] loved her—a frank, blustering fellow without guile enough to conceal his feelings, and no desire to do so. For two weeks past he had sought her society eagerly and persistently. She was confidently waiting for him to declare himself and she meant to accept him. The rather insignificant and unattractive Brantain was enormously rich; and she liked and required the entourage which wealth could give her.

2. During one of the pauses between their talk of the last tea and the next reception the door opened and a young man entered whom Brantain knew quite well. The girl turned her face toward him. A stride or two brought him to her side, and bending over her chair—before she could suspect his intention, for she did not realize that he had not seen her visitor—he pressed an ardent, lingering kiss upon her lips.

3. Brantain slowly arose; so did the girl arise, but quickly, and the newcomer stood between them, a little amusement and some defiance struggling with the confusion in his face.

4. "I believe," stammered Brantain, "I see that I have stayed too long. I—I had no idea—that is, I must wish you good-by." He . . . probably did not perceive that she was extending her hand to him, her presence of mind had not completely deserted her; but she could not have trusted herself to speak.

5. "Hang me if I saw him sitting there, Nattie! I know it's awkward for you. But I hope you'll forgive me this once. . . . Why, what's the matter?"

6. "Don't touch me; don't come near me," she returned angrily. "What do you mean by entering the house without ringing?"

7. "I came in with your brother, as I often do," he answered coldly, in self-justification. "We came in the side way. He went upstairs and I came in here hoping to find you. The explanation is simple enough and ought to satisfy you that the misadventure was unavoidable. But do say that you forgive me, Nathalie," he entreated, softening.

8. "Forgive you! . . . Let me pass. It depends upon—a good deal whether I ever forgive you."

9. At that next reception which she and Brantain had been talking about she approached the young man with a delicious frankness of manner when she saw him there.

10. "Will you let me speak to you a moment or two, Mr. Brantain?" she asked with an engaging but perturbed[12] smile. He seemed extremely unhappy; but

---

[12] perturbed: worried

when she took his arm and walked away with him, seeking a retired[13] corner, a ray of hope mingled with the almost comical misery of his expression. She was apparently very outspoken.

11   "Perhaps I should not have sought this interview, Mr. Brantain; but—but, oh, I have been very uncomfortable, almost miserable since that little encounter the other afternoon. When I thought how you might have misinterpreted it, and believed things"—hope was plainly gaining [the ascendancy] over misery in Brantain's round, guileless[14] face— "Of course, I know it is nothing to you, but for my own sake I do want you to understand that Mr. Harvy is an intimate friend of long standing. Why, we have always been like cousins—like brother and sister, I may say. He is my brother's most intimate associate and often fancies that he is entitled to the same privileges as the family. Oh, I know it is absurd, uncalled for, to tell you this; undignified even," she was almost weeping, "but it makes so much difference to me what you think of—of me." . . . The misery had all disappeared from Brantain's face.

12   "Then you do really care what I think, Miss Nathalie? May I call you Miss Nathalie?" They turned into a long, dim corridor. . . . They walked slowly to the very end of it. When they turned to retrace their steps Brantain's face was radiant and hers was triumphant.

13   Harvy was among the guests at the wedding; and he sought her out in a rare moment when she stood alone.

14   "Your husband," he said, smiling, "has sent me over to kiss you."

15   A quick blush suffused her face and round polished throat. "I suppose it's natural for a man to feel and act generously on an occasion of this kind. He tells me he doesn't want his marriage to interrupt . . . that pleasant intimacy which has existed between you and me. I don't know what you've been telling him," with an insolent smile, "but he has sent me here to kiss you."

16   She felt like a chess player who, by the clever handling of his pieces, sees the game taking the course intended. Her eyes were bright and tender with a smile as they glanced up into his; and her lips looked hungry for the kiss which they invited.

17   "But, you know," he went on quietly, "I didn't tell him so, it would have seemed ungrateful, but I can tell you. I've stopped kissing women; it's dangerous."

18   Well, she had Brantain and his million left. A person can't have everything in this world; and it was a little unreasonable of her to expect it.

21. Which statement *best* states a theme of the story?

    A. The best marriages are between equals.
    B. Old family friends are the most loyal.
    C. Love is a game played mostly by fools.
    D. People rarely get everything they want.

---

[13] retired: off to one side or concealed
[14] guileless: innocent rather than deceitful

22. Based on the details in paragraph 13, what most likely happened in paragraph 12 when they walked to the end of the corridor?

    A. Brantain refused to accept Nathalie's apology.
    B. Brantain traveled far away to forget Nathalie.
    C. Brantain proposed marriage to Nathalie.
    D. Brantain demanded that Nathalie change.

Use the following excerpt to answer Question 23:

She felt like a chess player who, by the clever handling of his pieces, sees the game taking the course intended.

23. What does the comparison of Nathalie to a chess player reveal about her?

    A. She excels at playing board games.
    B. She controls her situation completely.
    C. She enjoys intellectual challenges.
    D. She considers herself a good sport.

Use the following excerpt to answer Question 24:

He is my brother's most intimate associate and often fancies that he is entitled to the same privileges as the family.

24. Which of the following words could replace *intimate* in the sentence without changing its meaning?

    A. faithful
    B. cozy
    C. secret
    D. familiar

25. Based on the details in paragraph 18, what inference can you make about what might happen next?

    A. Nathalie will respond to losing Harvy by enjoying her new wealth.
    B. Nathalie will pursue Harvy's love despite being a married woman.
    C. Nathalie will be heartbroken by Harvy's surprising rejection of her.
    D. Nathalie will punish Harvy by building a happy life with Brantain.

Use the passage to answer Questions 26–30.

Excerpted from *The Red Badge of Courage* by Stephen Crane

1. The youth thought the damp fog of early morning moved from the rush of a great body of troops. From the distance came a sudden spatter of firing.

2. He was bewildered. As he ran with his comrades he strenuously tried to think, but all he knew was that if he fell down those coming behind would tread upon him. All his faculties seemed to be needed to guide him over and past obstructions. He felt carried along by a mob.

3. The sun spread disclosing rays, and, one by one, regiments burst into view like armed men just born of the earth. The youth perceived that the time had come. He was about to be measured. For a moment he felt in the face of his great trial like a babe, and the flesh over his heart seemed very thin. He seized time to look about him calculatingly.

4. But he instantly saw that it would be impossible for him to escape from the regiment. It enclosed him. And there were iron laws of tradition and law on four sides. He was in a moving box.

5. As he perceived this fact it occurred to him that he had never wished to come to the war. He had not enlisted of his free will. He had been dragged by the merciless government. And now they were taking him out to be slaughtered.

6. The regiment slid down a bank and wallowed across a little stream. The mournful current moved slowly on, and from the water, shaded black, some white bubble eyes looked at the men.

7. As they climbed the hill on the farther side artillery began to boom. Here the youth forgot many things as he felt a sudden impulse of curiosity. He scrambled up the bank with a speed that could not be exceeded by a bloodthirsty man.

8. He expected a battle scene.

9. There were some little fields girted[15] and squeezed by a forest. Spread over the grass and in among the tree trunks, he could see knots and waving lines of skirmishers who were running hither and thither and firing at the landscape. A dark battle line lay upon a sunstruck clearing that gleamed orange color. A flag fluttered.

10. Other regiments floundered up the bank. The brigade was formed in line of battle, and after a pause started slowly through the woods in the rear of the receding skirmishers,[16] who were continually melting into the scene to appear again farther on. They were always busy as bees, deeply absorbed in their little combats.

---

[15] girted: closely encircled
[16] skirmishers: soldiers engaged in skirmishes, or short bursts of combat

11 The youth tried to observe everything. He did not use care to avoid trees and branches, and his forgotten feet were constantly knocking against stones or getting entangled in briars. He was aware that these battalions with their commotions were woven red and startling into the gentle fabric of softened greens and browns. It looked to be a wrong place for a battle field.

Use the following excerpt to answer Question 26:

The youth perceived that the time had come. He was about to be measured.

26. In this context, the word *measured* means _____.

    A. tested
    B. killed
    C. planned
    D. weighed

27. Which is the *best* summary of paragraph 3? When the sun comes out the young man

    A. can see all the regiments around him. He knows it is time to fight but he feels sick.
    B. understands he is about to undergo a trial. He feels defenseless and sizes up his situation.
    C. knows that a great battle is about to begin. He prepares to run away secretly.
    D. looks around him and sees the regiments gathering in the distance. He is ready to fight.

Use the following excerpt to answer Question 28.

The youth tried to observe everything. He did not use care to avoid trees and branches, and his forgotten feet were constantly knocking against stones or getting entangled in briars. He was aware that these battalions with their commotions were woven red and startling into the gentle fabric of softened greens and browns. It looked to be a wrong place for a battle field.

28. Based on the final paragraph, what is the theme of the entire passage?

    A. War requires bravery.
    B. War inspires true patriotism.
    C. War is a necessary evil.
    D. War is a disturbing force.

29. What is the purpose of the details in paragraphs 9–10?

    A. They show how organized and brave the soldiers are.
    B. They contrast each army's fighting style on the field.
    C. They portray the troops' actions as small and insignificant.
    D. They convey the author's feelings about the uselessness of war.

30. What conclusion can you draw about the youth's relationship to the battle?

    A. It is a frightening situation that he doubts he will escape alive.
    B. It is an experience far different from what he expected.
    C. It is an opportunity to prove his manhood to his fellow soldiers.
    D. It is a life-changing occasion that he cannot understand.

Use the passage to answer Questions 31–35.

Adapted from *Winesburg, Ohio* by Sherwood Anderson

1   All through his boyhood and young manhood George Willard had been in the habit of walking on Trunion Pike. He had been in the midst of the great open place on winter nights when it was covered with snow and only the moon looked down at him; he had been there in the fall when bleak winds blew and on summer evenings when the air vibrated with the song of insects. On the April morning he wanted to go there again, to walk again in the silence. He did walk to where the road dipped down by a little stream two miles from town and then turned and walked silently back again. When he got to Main Street clerks were sweeping the sidewalks before the stores. "Hey, you George. How does it feel to be going away?" they asked.

2   The westbound train leaves Winesburg at seven forty-five in the morning. . . .

3   George came down the little incline from the New Willard House at seven o'clock. Tom Willard carried his bag. The son had become taller than the father.

4   On the station platform everyone shook the young man's hand. More than a dozen people waited about. Then they talked of their own affairs. Even Will Henderson, who was lazy and often slept until nine, had got out of bed. George was embarrassed. Gertrude Wilmot, a tall thin woman of fifty who worked in the Winesburg post office, came along the station platform. She had never before paid any attention to George. Now she stopped and put out her hand. In two words she voiced what everyone felt. "Good luck," she said sharply and then turning went on her way.

5   When the train came into the station George felt relieved. He scampered hurriedly aboard. Helen White came running along Main Street hoping to have a parting word with him, but he had found a seat and did not see her. When the train started Tom Little punched his ticket, grinned and, although he knew George well and knew on what adventure he was just setting out, made no comment. Tom had seen a thousand George Willards go out of their towns to the city. It was a commonplace enough incident with him. In the smoking car there was a man who had just invited Tom to go on a fishing trip to Sandusky Bay. He wanted to accept the invitation and talk over details.

6   George glanced up and down the car to be sure no one was looking, then took out his pocket-book and counted his money. His mind was occupied with a desire not to appear green. Almost the last words his father had said to him concerned the matter of his behavior when he got to the city. "Be a sharp one," Tom Willard had said. "Keep your eyes on your money. Be awake. That's the ticket. Don't let anyone think you're a greenhorn."[17]

---

[17] greenhorn: an inexperienced or ignorant person

7   After George counted his money he looked out of the window and was surprised to see that the train was still in Winesburg.

8   The young man, going out of his town to meet the adventure of life, began to think but he did not think of anything very big or dramatic. Things like his mother's death, his departure from Winesburg, the uncertainty of his future life in the city, the serious and larger aspects of his life did not come into his mind.

9   He thought of little things—Turk Smollet wheeling boards through the main street of his town in the morning, a tall woman, beautifully gowned, who had once stayed overnight at his father's hotel, Butch Wheeler the lamp lighter of Winesburg hurrying through the streets on a summer evening and holding a torch in his hand, Helen White standing by a window in the Winesburg post office and putting a stamp on an envelope.

10 The young man's mind was carried away by his growing passion for dreams. One looking at him would not have thought him particularly sharp. With the recollection of little things occupying his mind he closed his eyes and leaned back in the car seat. He stayed that way for a long time and when he aroused himself and again looked out of the car window the town of Winesburg had disappeared and his life there had become but a background on which to paint the dreams of his manhood.

31. In paragraph 4, what can you infer about the townspeople's reaction to George's departure?

    A. They feel excited for him.
    B. They anticipate his failure.
    C. They are angry to see him go.
    D. They delight in his misfortune.

Use the following excerpt to answer Question 32.

His mind was occupied with a desire not to appear green.

32. What does this sentence tell you about George?

    A. He is delighted to be leaving his hometown.
    B. He is feeling ill and hopes no one else notices.
    C. He is worried about what people think of him.
    D. He is well prepared for his adventure in the city.

33. The details George remembers in paragraph 9 show

    A. how a small town is a place with good values.
    B. how brief impressions can have strong meaning.
    C. how the townspeople lead sad, repressed lives.
    D. how a humble existence is the most rewarding.

34. Which of the following events occurs last in the story?

    A. George realizes that the train has left Winesburg.
    B. George counts the money in his pocket-book.
    C. George plans to go fishing with another man.
    D. George walks along Trunion Pike in silence.

Use the following excerpt to answer Question 35.

One looking at him would not have thought him particularly sharp.

35. Which word would change the tone of the sentence if it replaced the word *sharp*?

    A. intelligent
    B. shrewd
    C. alert
    D. bitter

Use the passage to answer Questions 36–40.

Adapted from *Summer* by Edith Wharton

1   A girl came out of lawyer Royall's house, at the end of the one street of North Dormer, and stood on the doorstep. . . .

2   The little June wind, frisking down the street, shook the doleful fringes of the Hatchard spruces, caught the straw hat of a young man just passing under them, and spun it clean across the road into the duck-pond.

3   As he ran to fish it out the girl on lawyer Royall's doorstep noticed that he was a stranger, that he wore city clothes, and that he was laughing with all his teeth, as the young and careless laugh at such mishaps.

4   Her heart contracted a little, and the shrinking that sometimes came over her when she saw people with holiday faces made her draw back into the house and pretend to look for the key that she knew she had already put into her pocket. A narrow greenish mirror with a gilt eagle over it hung on the passage wall, and she looked critically at her reflection, wished for the thousandth time that she had blue eyes like Annabel Balch, the girl who sometimes came from Springfield to spend a week with old Miss Hatchard, straightened the sunburnt hat over her small swarthy face, and turned out again into the sunshine.

5   "How I hate everything!" she murmured.

6   The young man had passed through the Hatchard gate, and she had the street to herself. North Dormer is at all times an empty place, and at three o'clock on a June afternoon its few able-bodied men are off in the fields or woods, and the women indoors, engaged in languid[18] household drudgery.

7   The girl walked along, swinging her key on a finger, and looking about her with the heightened attention produced by the presence of a stranger in a familiar place. What, she wondered, did North Dormer look like to people from other parts of the world? She herself had lived there since the age of five, and had long supposed it to be a place of some importance. But about a year before, Mr. Miles, the new Episcopal clergyman at Hepburn, . . . had proposed, in a fit of missionary zeal, to take the young people down to Nettleton to hear an illustrated lecture on the Holy Land. . . .

8   In the course of that incredible day Charity Royall had, for the first and only time, experienced railway-travel, looked into shops with plate-glass fronts, tasted coconut pie, sat in a theater, and listened to a gentleman saying unintelligible things before pictures that she would have enjoyed looking at if his explanations had not prevented her from understanding them. This initiation had shown her that North Dormer was a small place, and developed in her a thirst for information that her position as custodian[19] of the village library had previously failed to excite. For a month or two

---

[18] languid: slow-paced
[19] custodian: caretaker

she dipped feverishly and disconnectedly into the dusty volumes of the Hatchard Memorial Library; then the impression of Nettleton began to fade, and she found it easier to take North Dormer as the norm of the universe than to go on reading.

9   She had been "brought down from the Mountain." . . . Charity was not very clear about the Mountain; but she knew it was a bad place, and a shame to have come from, and that, whatever befell her in North Dormer, she ought, as Miss Hatchard had once reminded her, to remember that she had been brought down from there, and hold her tongue and be thankful. She looked up at the Mountain, thinking of these things, and tried as usual to be thankful.

10 But the sight of the young man turning in at Miss Hatchard's gate had brought back the vision of the glittering streets of Nettleton, and she felt ashamed of her old sun-hat, and sick of North Dormer, and jealously aware of Annabel Balch of Springfield, opening her blue eyes somewhere far off on glories greater than the glories of Nettleton.

11 "How I hate everything!" she said again.

36. How does the story's setting affect Charity Royall?

   A. It excites her.
   B. It saddens her.
   C. It irritates her.
   D. It impresses her.

37. Which of the following two words describe the town of North Dormer? Write them in the blank circles below. (**Note**: On the actual GED® test, you will click on each word and "drag" it into position in the organizer.)

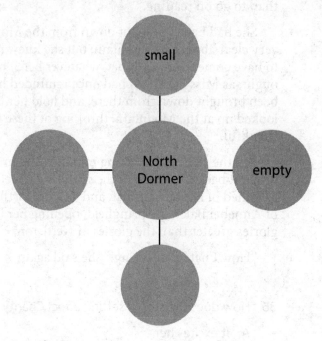

A. urban
B. dull
C. backward
D. overcrowded
E. gossipy

38. What is the connection between Charity Royall and the young man?

A. They are former classmates; his studies in the city inspire Charity to leave the small town.
B. They are total strangers; his appearance makes Charity feel dissatisfied with her life in North Dormer.
C. They are distant cousins; his arrival upsets Charity by reminding her of life on the mountain.
D. They are old friends; his good looks and sense of humor inspire Charity's mood to improve.

39. Which is the *best* summary of paragraph 8?

    A. A visit to a nearby town makes Charity realize the insignificance of her hometown. She tries to broaden her mind through reading but soon gives up.
    B. Charity visits nearby Nettleton where she shops, eats at a restaurant, and goes to a museum. Afterward, North Dormer seems dull.
    C. Charity's visit to a nearby town makes her hungry for books. She reads as many as she can before admitting she does not care for reading.
    D. A visit to a nearby town gives Charity an opportunity to see a different life for herself. Later, she dreams of living in a large city.

40. What is the meaning of the word *impression* as it is used in paragraph 8?

    A. mark
    B. print
    C. thought
    D. opinion

CHAPTER 5
Extended Response

The Extended Response item on the GED® Reasoning through Language Arts test requires you to analyze one or more texts in order to create a writing sample. Because you will be typing your response into a computer, you will be able to write down your ideas quickly, and then go back to refine your writing. As you write, you will be able to view the passages that you are writing about, which will help you recall their arguments and the evidence they contain.

You have 45 minutes to plan, draft, and revise your response. You will be tested for these skills:

- how well you analyze arguments, including your ability to provide relevant and sufficient evidence to support your analysis

- how well you develop and organize your writing so it flows logically and coherently

- how well you demonstrate the ability to edit and understand standard American English for clarity and correctness

Extended Response 1

Directions

The following article presents arguments for and against the rise of technology in everyday life.

In your response, analyze both positions to determine which one is most persuasive and best supported. Use relevant and specific evidence from the arguments to support your response. You should expect to spend up to 45 minutes planning, drafting, and editing your response. Write or type your response on a separate sheet of paper. (**Note:** *On the real GED® test you will type your response onto a computer screen.*)

1   Technology's influence is everywhere today, from our workplaces to our homes. In fact, technology, especially in the form of cell phones, tablets, and personal computers, now defines most areas of daily life, such as how people work, shop, and socialize. This raises the question of whether the rise of technology is more of an advantage than a disadvantage.

2   Many companies, for example, are integrating technology into the workplace, such as by giving employees tablets. This promotes speed and flexibility. On the other hand, technology makes workers accessible around the clock to their bosses. This caused France to pass a law forbidding managers from contacting their employees outside of work hours by cell phone or email.

Arguments in Favor of the Rise of Technology

3   Instead of blaming technology, we need to recognize its benefits and adapt. In fact, civilization has always had to adapt to technological change. There were also complaints when the car, the telephone, and the printing press were invented that they would change life for the worse. Now, we take them for granted. We will adapt to the latest technological revolution, too.

4   In addition, technology has opened up a whole new world of educational possibilities for ourselves and our children. A 2014 survey of middle school students found that 83 percent said that lessons incorporating technology, such as online games and research, would make them much more likely to be interested in a lesson.

5   The social benefits of technology are also clear. Opponents may claim that they are forced to keep up with too many emails and texts, but there is no question that technology makes it easier to keep in touch with loved ones and friends and makes communicating at work faster and easier.

This is especially important when parents need to keep track of their children, for example, or when employees work together on an important project. In fact, studies have shown that a higher percentage of Americans report that technology has brought them closer to friends and family than they had been before.

6   In addition, technology makes our lives outside of work easier. Functions such as GPS, electronic calendars, and others are less cumbersome than carrying printed materials. Recent studies have shown that over 90 percent of Americans now own a cell phone and over 65 percent own a tablet. There is no point arguing over what is now a fact of life and cannot be changed. Americans have clearly embraced technology because of its benefits, so everyone else should do the same.

Arguments against the Rise of Technology

7   Today's technology is destroying our quality of life. We wake up and start checking email messages. After skimming and answering the email, voicemail, and texts, we wolf down a power bar instead of eating a decent breakfast or spending time with our family, and we dash off to work. During our commute, we hook ourselves to a music player, although incoming calls or tweets constantly disrupt our concentration.

8   At work, we are deluged by information via email that needs to be absorbed quickly or requests for information that make us drop what we are doing to meet a colleague's demand. Meanwhile, we handle phone calls from customers who want quick resolution of their problems while we simultaneously email bosses who want instant answers to their questions.

9   Amid all the rushing, no one stops to ask whether slowing down and actually thinking about an issue might produce better answers. No one suggests that multitasking might not be quite as efficient or effective as doing one thing at a time and doing it right before moving on to the next. In fact, according to a recent study at Finn University, multitasking actually prevents complex problem solving and results in higher numbers of work errors.

10   Employers now expect us to be available at all times of the night and day via our cell phones and email. The U.S. Department of Labor reports that over 70 percent of American workers report using cell phones or other devices to stay in touch with their workplaces outside of work hours. What happened to privacy? What happened to family time?

11   This is taking a toll on us physically, mentally, and emotionally. The Centers for Disease Control and Prevention says that one-half of all Americans have hypertension. Doctors report increasing loss of vision and hearing due to the continuous use of electronic devices. We lack time to eat, exercise, or sleep properly. It is time to cut back on our use of technology and save our health and our sanity.

Extended Response 2

Directions

The following article contains arguments for and against state lotteries.

*In your response, analyze both positions to determine which one is most persuasive and best supported. Use relevant and specific evidence from the arguments to support your response. You should expect to spend up to 45 minutes planning, drafting, and editing your response. Write or type your response on a separate sheet of paper. (**Note:** On the real GED® test, you will type your response onto a computer screen.)*

State lotteries are familiar to almost everyone. A lottery is a gambling game run by a state. You may scratch a ticket to see if you have won a prize or guess a series of numbers and see if they match a combination of numbers produced at random.

The dream of instant wealth is a great temptation, and millions of people buy lottery tickets each year in the hope that their lives will be magically transformed. Lottery tickets are easily available at supermarkets and convenience stores and usually cost within the range of one to five dollars. Prizes can range from a few dollars to multiple millions.

However, lotteries have recently inspired debate about who really profits from them and whether lotteries are legitimate or just a way for states to generate funds at their residents' expense.

Argument against State Lotteries

1. States are stealing money from the poor, and they don't even have to ambush anyone. The unsuspecting poor hand their money over voluntarily when they desperately purchase lottery tickets in the false hope of striking it rich.

2. Who plays the lottery? Many players come from the poor, the uneducated, and those who are discriminated against. According to a government study, 54% of frequent lottery players have household incomes under $40,000. Many are high school dropouts. Studies show that the lower the income, the more likely a person is to play the lottery.

3. Lottery supporters say that the amounts people bet are small, just a dollar or two here or there. But a dollar or two every week takes a bite out of the meager income of someone living at or near the poverty level. On the other hand, the lottery means big profits for states. According to the Delman Business Institute, lotteries took in more than $50 *billion* in 2013. That is a lot of one- and two-dollar bets moving out of poor people's pockets.

4   Lottery supporters say that lotteries are better than taxes because people choose to buy the tickets *and* actually have a chance to benefit if they win. But the odds of winning a state lottery are as high as 150 million to one. Some reports say you're more likely to be hit by a car than win a state lottery. Supporters of the state lottery also try to justify it by noting that it supports vital programs such as education or care for the elderly. The truth is, state legislatures simply shift general revenue funds out of education and programs for the elderly knowing that the lottery proceeds will replace them. According to a recent federal government study, only a small fraction of the money actually goes to the programs.

5   Lotteries violate the government's most fundamental obligation: to promote the common good. They prey on the underprivileged, dangling the false promise of riches to come.

Argument in Favor of State Lotteries

6   Want to help your state have better schools? Want to provide transportation for the elderly or help them get needed medicines at reduced cost? If so, buy a lottery ticket. Critics of lotteries say that most players will not win and get nothing for the money they spend buying a ticket, but there are several benefits.

7   State lotteries have become an important part of state government, generating nearly $50 billion in 2013. They are extremely popular as well, with lottery programs found in 44 states, including the District of Columbia. The prevalence of lotteries also shows that they are popular with the public, who in many cases voted to approve the adoption of these games.

8   Those revenues can make a difference. California's schools gain half a million dollars in funding a year from its lottery. Pennsylvania's elderly benefited to the tune of $75 million in long-term care, rent subsidies, transportation, subsidized medicines, and senior centers because of lotteries. As a result, these lottery revenues spare taxpayers.

9   Critics say that most people will not win the lottery. However, lottery purchases are voluntary purchases with the potential for reward. That potential is real: in one recent year, more than 500 players won more than a $1 million, and more than 4,500 more took jackpots of $100,000 or more. Thousands and thousands more players won smaller jackpots that could have been enough to treat their families to a restaurant meal or buy school supplies.

ANSWERS AND EXPLANATIONS

Chapter 1: Grammar and Conventions

1. Choice **C** is correct because it correctly places commas after each of the items in a series.

2. Choice **A** is correct because it shows the appropriate end marks in each sentence. Choice B does not present the proper tone for a community memo.

3. Choice **D** is correct. It shows the correct use of the pronoun *it* to refer to the singular word *garden* in the previous sentence.

4. Choice **C** is correct because it shows the correct use of an apostrophe to show the possessive form of *anyone else*: *anyone else's*.

5. Choice **C** is correct because it is uses parallel construction for the verbs *experience*, *enjoy*, and *grow*.

6. Choice **D** is correct because it uses the conjunctive adverb *however* to indicate a contrast with the idea in the previous clause.

7. Choice **A** is correct because it is the only choice in which the modifier *first* is placed next to the verb it modifies: *learn*.

8. Choice **C** is correct. It expresses the ideas in a clear and concise way without creating a run-on sentence.

9. Choice **B** is correct. The pronoun *it* correctly refers to *the animal* in the previous sentence.

10. Choice **D** uses capitalization correctly. Days of the week should be capitalized, but the word *open* should not.

11. Choice **B** is correct because it is clear and concise. The other choices are wordy or have awkward construction.

12. Choice **B** is correct. It uses formal or Standard English, which is appropriate to a business letter, while the other choices do not.

13. Choice **C** correctly uses *me*, the objective form of the first person pronoun.

14. Choice **A** correctly uses the homonyms *two* and *to*.

15. Choice **C** is correct because it does not contain any misplaced modifiers.

16. Choice **D** is correct because it has the proper coordination of ideas joined by the coordinating conjunction *and*.

17. Choice **A** is correct because it correctly uses a comma to set off the introductory phrase.

18. Choice **C** is correct because it uses the proper coordinating conjunction *so*. *Hence* is an adverb.

19. Choice **B** is correct because *his or her* is the best use of pronouns to take the place of the singular *everyone*. Choice D is also singular, but not gender-neutral (which is preferred).

20. Choice **C** is correct because it uses punctuation and conjunctions to eliminate a run-on or fused sentence.

21. Choice **A** is correct. Its plural verbs are in agreement with their plural subjects: *employees/feel* and *companies/have*.

22. Choice **D** is correct. Unlike the other choices, choice D has a verb and it creates a complete sentence, rather than a fragment.

23. Choice **D** is correct because the conjunctive adverb *therefore* makes the most sense in the sentence.

24. Choice **A** is correct. The idiomatic expression is "up to me."

25. Choice **C** is correct. Its verbs are in agreement with its subjects: *what/is* and *brands/are*.

26. Choice **D** correctly uses an apostrophe to indicate the possessive form of the word *company*.

27. Choice **A** correctly uses the homonyms *there* and *no*.

ANSWERS AND EXPLANATIONS

28. Choice **B** is correct. The pronouns in the phrase *he or she* stand in for the singular antecedent *consumer*. The words *consumer*, *he*, and *she* are all singular, so the singular verb *is* is correct here.

29. Choice **C** is correct because it avoids informal or overblown language.

30. Choice **C** is correct because unlike the other answer choices, it is a complete sentence with a subject and a verb.

31. Choice **D** is correct. The words *news* and *activity* are singular nouns that require the singular forms of the verbs: *is* and *protects*.

32. Choice **B** is correct. It correctly places a comma between all the items in a series.

33. Choice **C** is correct because it uses the correct forms of the homonyms *your* and *weight*.

34. Choice **D** is correct. It is the only choice that uses a transitional word that suggests contrast.

35. Choice **A** correctly capitalizes the first word in the sentence and also the two proper nouns: *Madison* and *Longview*.

36. Choice **A** correctly uses the plural possessive form: *children's*.

37. Choice **B** is correct. An exclamation point is the most appropriate end mark for this sentence, which expresses great enthusiasm. Choices C and D do not use end marks and create fragments.

38. Choice **C** is correct. It is balanced and parallel. The listed items are all nouns in the gerund form.

39. Choice **B** is correct. It uses punctuation and the conjunction *and* to avoid creating a run-on sentence.

40. Choice **D** is correct. It is the only choice that is a complete sentence because it contains a subject and a verb.

Chapter 2: Informational Texts

1. Choice **D** is correct because several uses are discussed. Paragraphs 6 and 7 discuss many uses beyond the space program.

2. Choice **B** is correct. The passage discusses how the device is complex because of its technological innovations, multiple joints, and versatility.

3. **Benefits of the X1 in Space (discussed in paragraph 5):**

   A: The X1 can measure, record, and stream back data to Mission Control.

   D: The X1 can replicate crucial muscle-building exercises in microgravity.

   Benefits of the X1 on Earth (discussed in paragraphs 6 and 7):

   B: The X1 can assist wearers walking over varied terrain as well as on stairs.

   C: The X1 can provide paraplegics with physical support and motor function.

4. Choice **C** is correct. Paragraph 5 gives examples of how the X1 could be used in space and paragraph 6 gives examples of how the X1 could be used on Earth.

5. Choice **D** is correct. The X1 would be used in the microgravity of space to create resistance so that astronauts could maintain their muscle mass. On Earth, the X1 would be used to assist people who cannot use their muscles to stand and walk.

ANSWERS AND EXPLANATIONS

6. Choice **A** is correct. The word *change* has a neutral connotation since change could be good or bad.

7. Choice **C** is the most reasonable hypothesis. The paragraph discusses the successful development of the X1 so far, but it is also about the researchers' plan for future improvements to the device. The last line of the passage indicates this.

8. Choice **C** is correct. The word *impact* here means effect.

9. Choice **D** is correct. The pie chart and the first line of the text clearly show that petroleum is "the largest share of the US primary energy consumption."

10. Choice **C** is correct. The largest "piece" of the pie chart represents petroleum consumption, and the main idea of paragraph 1 is that oil makes up the largest share of consumption.

11. Choice **C** is correct. Paragraph 3 states that the United States produces only 84% of the energy it uses.

12. Choice **B** is correct. Line 1 states that the United States consumes more oil than any other primary energy source. The US is dependent on oil.

13. Choice **A** is correct. If US production of renewable energy sources has doubled since 1970, that would support the author's claim that energy production has recently changed.

14. Choice **C** is correct. The first three paragraphs focus on US energy consumption. The rest of the passage discusses US energy production.

15. Choice **C** is correct. The paragraph states that 92% of petroleum oil is used for transportation, which suggests that transportation is the main reason for oil consumption.

16. Choice **B** is correct. Paragraph 9 describes the increase in production of various types of renewable energy, such as wind and solar power.

17. Choice **C** is correct. *Comprehensive* is an adjective that means "total" or "complete."

18. The correct order is

    D First, your body releases hormones.

    A Then, your heart rate and breathing rate go up.

    C Next, your blood vessels narrow to restrict flow.

    B Finally, blood flows mostly to your muscles and heart.

19. Choice **D** is correct. The phrase "in contrast" is a transition after a paragraph about the effects of stress on the body. It allows the author to return to his or her main point about the benefits of relaxation techniques in the final paragraph.

20. Choice **A** is correct. The overall structure of the passage is cause-and-effect. It allows the author to consider the causes and effects of stress and relaxation techniques on the human body.

21. Choice **B** is correct. The author assumes that most people would prefer to live healthier and happier lives. He or she includes several lists of illnesses and conditions caused or exacerbated by stress in order to suggest that relaxation would reduce the symptoms of stress-related illness.

22. Choice **C** is correct. From the sentence, one can infer that relaxation has benefits for the mind and body.

23. Answers will vary. *Counteract* means "to lessen" or "to act against." Synonyms of this word may include, but are not limited to, *lessen*, *reduce*, *slow*, *neutralize*, *compensate*, and *prevent*.

ANSWERS AND EXPLANATIONS

24. Answers will vary. Antonyms, or words with the opposite meaning from *counteract*, may include, but are not limited to, *increase*, *contribute to*, and *speed up*.

25. Choice **B** is correct. Only the article, in paragraph 3, provides advice on reducing the risk of injury and avoiding excessive fatigue.

26. Choice **A** is correct. The chart extends the information in the preceding paragraph by describing the type and duration of moderate versus vigorous activities.

27. Choice **D** is correct. The third column of the chart provides instructions for exercising properly.

28. Choice **C** is correct. The guidelines are written in a more formal style than the fact sheet because they include full explanatory paragraphs, rather than the fact sheet's brief sentences and bulleted lists.

29. Choice **D** is correct because both give advice and stress the importance of exercise. This would not be necessary if Americans already got enough exercise.

30. Choice **B** is correct. Both passages suggest that Americans will experience health benefits if they exercise regularly.

31. Choice **C** is correct. Both passages suggest that physical activity provides adults with health benefits.

32. Choice **B** is correct. The word *hearty* is a synonym for *vigorous*.

33. Both passages inform readers about how to exercise properly.

34. Choice **A** is correct. The first paragraph describes how mounds are formed and the types of places they are generally located. The second paragraph discusses the specific regions near the author in which mounds are found. A is the best summary of the passage.

35. Choice **C** is correct. This statement is a conclusion drawn by the author, not a statement of proven fact.

36. Choice **B** is correct. The author most likely lives in northwest Canada. In the second paragraph, he refers to the area as *our Northwest* and mentions the *Canadian Pacific Hotel*.

37. Choice **A** is correct. When the author says *communication*, he means the way to travel from one river to another. *Ascending* means going up, so the sentence as a whole means that the way to travel from the Red River to the Rainy River is to go up the Red Lake River.

38. Choice **D** is correct. The first paragraph of the passage says, "The mounds are as a rule found in the midst of a fertile section of country, and it is pretty certain from this that the mound builders were agriculturists."

39. Choice **B** is correct. The passage describes the mounds as having round or elliptical bases with either flattened or slightly rounded tops. The first sentence describes them as flattened cones.

40. Choice **A** is correct. The passage is mostly description of the mounds, and the second paragraph of the passage says, "Our Northwest has, however, been neglected in the accounts of the mound-bearing region." Therefore, the author's purpose is most likely to provide an account of the mounds to contribute to scholarship about them. The best answer is A.

ANSWERS AND EXPLANATIONS

Chapter 3: Argumentation and Persuasion

1. Choice **C** is correct. In the opening paragraph, the writer lists the benefits of educating women: "... their families are healthier, they have fewer children, they wed later, and they have more opportunities to generate income."

2. Choice **B** is correct. The author begins her argument by stating in the first paragraph several facts about how education benefits women, girls, and their families. She also states that there are still disparities, and that 3.6 million more girls are out of school and two-thirds of women are illiterate.

3. Choice **A** is correct. It is the only sentence that contains statistics that support the claim that educating women and girls has clear benefits.

4. Choice **C** is correct. The author cites statistics provided by the World Bank.

5. Choice **D** is correct. Paragraph 5 explains that the poor quality of education means that although many more women and girls go to school, some still do not learn to read. The author suggests that "a focus on both the quality of education and enrollment rates is needed."

6. Choice **B** is correct. The author is clearly enthusiastic about the benefits of educating women and girls around the world because of the benefits to their families and communities, despite her acknowledgement that improvements to women's education still need to be made.

7. Choice **C** is correct because it is the only choice that mentions an environmental issue: pollution.

8. Choice **D** is correct. The transition word *second* indicates that the writer is shifting to a discussion of a new idea.

9. Choice **B** is correct. The first writer is optimistic about driverless cars and lists several of their potential benefits. The second writer suggests several potential negative effects.

10. Choice **A** accurately describes the two writers' contrasting opinions about the driverless car. The first writer sees benefits, including reduced congestion on the roads; the second sees drawbacks, including increased congestion.

11. Choice **B** is correct. The writer claims in paragraph 1 that the driverless car will negatively affect the economy but never develops the point or provides evidence to support it.

12. Choice **C** is correct. The excerpt is about driverless cars. The evidence the writer provides here suggests that humans are prone to mistakes and that computers will be much better drivers.

13. Choice **D** is correct. The writer uses the phrase *Some say that* to acknowledge another point of view.

14. Choice **B** is correct. Both writers use a point-by-point structure for their arguments. Both writers uses transition words—*first, second, finally, most importantly*—to indicate the order of importance of these points.

15. Choice **C** is correct. In the first paragraph, President Clinton traces the "promise of America" through its birth and early development in the 18th and 19th centuries. In the second paragraph, he continues to explore its development during the 20th century.

16. Choice **B** is correct. Paragraphs 2, 3, and 5 include lists of historical actions that illustrate American's determination and promise.

17. Choice **C** is correct. In the first sentence of the paragraph, President Clinton expresses the idea that four years prior, "our march to this new future seemed less certain than it does

ANSWERS AND EXPLANATIONS

today." Later in the paragraph, he says, "our economy is the strongest on Earth."

18. Choice **D** is correct because the purpose of paragraph 6 is to explain what good government should do.

19. Choice **A** is correct. The paragraph focuses on the choices Americans must make as they and their nation face a new century.

20. Choice **B** is correct. President Clinton uses the phrase "American Century" in order to show the United States' importance in the world during the 20th century.

21. Choice **A** is correct. *Scourge* is a word with serious connotations. It means "the cause of great suffering." By using it, Clinton clearly communicates that he understands the serious role of slavery in America's past.

22. Choice **C** is correct. Clinton's inaugural speech is intended to usher in a new term. The president wants to inspire people as they move forward into the unknown.

23. Choice **B** is correct. The whistles are a metaphor for useless things that people value too much, such as popularity and wealth.

24. Answers will vary. Paragraphs 5 through 10 relate Franklin's observations of men and women who sacrificed their values—their freedom, their self-respect, their minds—in order to attain something not worth having. These examples include a man who desired the favor of the court, a man who coveted popularity, a miser, a hedonist, a spendthrift, and a woman who married a brute.

25. Choice **A** is correct. Franklin's purpose for writing is to provide evidence of people who suffer because of bad choices in order to persuade them to be more thoughtful.

26. Choice **C** is correct. The three paragraphs use a narrative structure to tell Franklin's childhood story; it provides background in support of his claim that people too often place too much value on things.

27. Choice **B** is correct. Franklin implies that if people were more thoughtful about the choices they make and the value they place on things and experiences, they would be less unhappy.

28. Answers will vary but may include *frustration*, *annoyance*, or *anger*.

29. Answers will vary but may include *thought*, *idea*, or *consideration*.

30. The correct answer is *reflection*. *Vexation* and *chagrin* both have negative connotations. *Reflection* is a neutral word.

31. Choice **B** is correct. In paragraphs 3 and 4, Ford claims that Congress has focused on conservation and done nothing to stimulate production of energy, such as passing laws to increase domestic oil and coal production.

32. Choice **C** is correct. The United States' dependency on foreign oil is the detail that supports Ford's claim that America is facing an energy problem.

33. Choice **A** is correct. Paragraph 9 explains that the measures in paragraphs 7 and 8 would "prevent unfair gains by oil companies . . . , furnish a substantial incentive to increase domestic energy production, and encourage conservation."

34. Explicit Purpose: **A**: Ford states directly that he blames Congress for its inaction in response to the energy problem; Implicit Purpose: **B**: Ford implies that the United States is falling behind other countries in energy technology.

35. Choice **B** is correct. In paragraph 7 of Ford's speech, he says that an import fee will "further discourage the consumption of imported fuel." In paragraph 3 of the second passage, Udall lists how Ford's proposals will actually drive up oil and gas prices.

ANSWERS AND EXPLANATIONS

36. Choice **D** is correct. In paragraph 3, Udall lists how Ford's proposals will drive up the prices of gasoline, electricity, and oil. In paragraph 5, he identifies the factors that Ford "ignores," such as the environmental impact of additional oil production.

37. Choice **C** is correct. Ford mentions that "Our American economy runs on energy—no energy, no jobs," but he does not provide examples or data to support this claim.

38. Choice **B** is correct. The tone of both speeches is one of urgency.

39. Choice **A** is correct. Paragraphs 9 and 10 show that Ford thinks it will help reduce US dependence on foreign oil and create jobs.

40. Choice **C** is correct. The last line of the passage shows that Udall thinks having more energy produced will make Americans continue to expect inexpensive and abundant energy supplies.

41. Choice **A** is correct. In paragraph 5, Udall differentiates his position from Ford's by stating that Ford's goal to increase production is unrealistic.

42. Choice **B** is correct. By repeating the word *down* in the third sentence, Ford reinforces the idea that oil production is falling.

Chapter 4: Literature

1. Choice **A** is correct. When Darcy refuses to dance with the other ladies, he causes conflict between himself and Bingley, who wishes Darcy to dance, and with the locals in the crowd, who begin to think Darcy is arrogant.

2. Choice **B** is correct. Elizabeth is quick to turn a slight by Mr. Darcy into a witty anecdote at Darcy's expense.

3. Choice **C** is correct. The word *ignored* is a synonym for *slighted*.

4. The correct order is **A, D, B, C**.

5. Choice **C** is correct. The first paragraph states that they are friends, but Mr. Darcy has the upper hand in the relationship; he is not easily swayed by his friend, as evidenced by his refusal to dance.

6. Choice **D** is correct. John is outwardly polite when his friends' fathers make remarks about his hometown, but privately he thinks critically of them.

7. Choice **B** is correct. Until this point, the story has focused on John and his thoughts. The story changes direction when Percy reveals his character to John by revealing his father's wealth.

8. Choice **C** is correct. John does not want to seem to offend his new friend, but he wants more information.

9. Choice **D** is correct. By mentioning the jewels, John wants to impress Percy with the amount of wealth he has seen.

10. Choice **B** is correct. The boys' friendship is based on their mutual interest in wealth, particularly jewels.

11. Choice **C** is correct. The details in paragraph 2 suggest that Mary is "not an affectionate child and had never cared much for anyone." She was "a little girl no one was very fond of."

ANSWERS AND EXPLANATIONS

12. Choice **B** is correct. Paragraph 2 reveals that the story begins after a cholera epidemic has killed all the adults who were caring for Mary.

13. Choice **B** is correct. Barney clearly feels pity for Mary, but he winks back his tears. This signals readers that they should feel sorry for Mary, who is now an orphan.

14. Choice **A** is correct. Mary and the snake are both alone, without assistance.

15. Choice **D** is correct. *Gently* would indicate that Mary is vulnerable or submissive instead of proud and arrogant.

16. Man: **B, C, F**; Dog: **A, D, E**.

17. Choice **B** is correct. The fact that the man's spittle turns instantly to brittle ice indicates the severity of the cold.

18. Choice **D** is correct. The narrator says that the thought that the severe cold might be dangerous never occurs to the man.

19. Choice **C** is correct. *Frailty* suggests weakness, not strength.

20. Choice **C** is correct. Paragraph 5 says, "Its instinct told it a truer tale than was told to the man by the man's judgment."

21. Choice **D** is correct. In the final lines of the story, the narrator states the theme directly: "A person can't have everything in this world; and it was a little unreasonable of her to expect it."

22. Choice **C** is correct. Brantain must have proposed to Nathalie because they are married in the following paragraph.

23. Choice **B** is correct. Like a chess master, Nathalie is in complete control of the game of love.

24. Choice **D** is correct. The word *familiar* is the synonym for *intimate* that makes the most sense in the sentence.

25. Choice **A** is correct. In the final sentence, the narrator suggests that in Nathalie's mind, Brantain's millions are a fair exchange for the attentions of Harvy. If she feels any pangs of regret about losing Harvy, she will overcome her loss by enjoying the wealth she gains through marriage.

26. Choice **A** is correct. In this sentence, the word *tested* is the best synonym for *measured*.

27. Choice **B** is correct. This summary includes all the key points in the correct order.

28. Choice **D** is correct. The theme of the passage is expressed in the final paragraph: "The battalions with their commotions" look "red and startling" and out of place in the countryside. "It looked to be a wrong place for a battle field." The war disturbs the peaceful landscape.

29. Choice **C** is correct. In paragraph 8, the youth expects a battle. In paragraphs 9 and 10, the narrator describes what the youth actually sees during the battle—scattered soldiers fighting "little" combats like busy insects.

30. Choice **B** is correct. The last line of the passage suggests that war is very different from what the young man expected.

31. Choice **A** is correct. The townspeople are excited for George and wish him well in his new life in the city.

32. Choice **C** is correct. George is worried that he will appear "green" or to act as a "greenhorn."

33. Choice **B** is correct. George's memories of the people are "of little things," but they are the ones he most remembers as he gets ready to leave town.

34. Choice **A** is correct. At the end of the story, George is surprised that the train has left Winesburg without his awareness.

35. Choice **D** is correct. In the story, *sharp* means "clever." *Bitter* is a synonym for a different

ANSWERS AND EXPLANATIONS

meaning of *sharp*—a strong, often unpleasant feeling. Using *bitter* this way would completely change the meaning of the sentence.

36. Choice **C** is correct. Although Charity had, as a child, thought the town of North Dormer was a place of importance, she has since discovered that it is a dull place. It irritates her.

37. Choice **B**: dull; Choice **C**: backward.

38. Choice **B** is correct. Charity and the young man are strangers. His presence in the town reminds her of a past visit to a larger, more exciting place, which increases her sense of dissatisfaction.

39. Choice **A** is correct. It mentions the key points only and in the correct order.

40. Choice **C** is correct. A synonym for *impression* is *thought*.

Chapter 5: Extended Response

If possible, ask an instructor to evaluate your essay. Your instructor's opinions and comments will help you determine what skills you need to practice in order to improve your writing skills.

You may also want to evaluate your essay yourself using the checklist that follows. The more items you can check, the more confident you can be about your writing skills. Items that are not checked will show you the essay-writing skills that you need to work on.

My essay:

- ☐ Creates a sound, logical argument based on the passage.
- ☐ Cites evidence from the passage to support the argument.
- ☐ Analyzes the issue and/or evaluates the validity of the arguments in the passage.
- ☐ Organizes ideas in a sensible sequence.
- ☐ Shows clear connections between main ideas.
- ☐ Uses largely correct sentence structure.
- ☐ Follows Standard English conventions in regard to grammar, spelling, and punctuation.

POSTTEST

Reasoning through Language Arts

This Posttest is intended to give you an idea of how ready you are to take the real GED® Reasoning through Language Arts Test. Try to work on each question in a quiet area so you are free from distractions, and give yourself enough time. The time allotted for the Posttest is 150 minutes, but it is more important to be sure you get a chance to think about every question than it is to finish ahead of time. The GED® Reasoning through Language Arts Test also includes a written-response section, known as the Extended Response. See Chapter 5 for two examples of that component of the test.

Answers and explanations for each question can be found at the end of the Posttest.

Part 1: 22 questions | **35 minutes**

The following letter from a job applicant contains several numbered blanks, each marked "Select... ▼" Beneath each one is a set of choices. Indicate the choice from each set that is correct and belongs in the blank. (Note: On the real GED® test, the choices will appear as a "drop-down" menu. When you click on a choice, it will appear in the blank.)

Marco Santori
Manager
Flotsam Automotive, Inc.
224 Bolsa Ave.
San Diego, CA 92888

Dear Mr. Santori:

    I read your 1. Select... ▼ I am writing to apply for a sales position at your dealership. I have enclosed my résumé for your review as well as three letters of reference. I am available to work immediately.

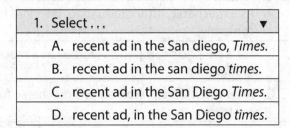

1. Select... ▼
A. recent ad in the San diego, *Times*.
B. recent ad in the san diego *times*.
C. recent ad in the San Diego *Times*.
D. recent ad, in the San Diego *times*.

127

POSTTEST

I have always been a car enthusiast. From an early age, I took careful note of [2. Select...▼] I worked for [3. Select...▼] We repaired foreign and domestic models, and I learned how a car works from the inside out.

2. Select... ▼
A. car makes and models, by the time I was ten, I could instantly identify almost any car.
B. car makes and models. By the time I was ten, I could instantly identify almost any car.
C. car makes and models by the time I was ten, I could instantly identify almost any car.
D. car makes and models. By the time I was ten. I could instantly identify almost any car.

3. Select... ▼
A. my cousins at their garage.
B. my cousin's at his or her garage.
C. my cousins' at their garage.
D. my cousins at his or her garage.

While I have not worked at a car dealership before, I have several years of sales experience. During college, I spent three years working in the Sales Department of a large furniture company, where I won an award for making the most sales annually. During my senior year, I took a job for a local technology company in a store that sells cell phones and cell phone plans. [4. Select...▼] This position also required frequent interaction with the public, and it was in many ways a sales-based position. I have received excellent feedback from the customers and clients I serviced. However, I recently left this position to pursue a career with a greater focus on sales.

4. Select... ▼
A. As a mechanic, after graduating, I worked for a car parts company.
B. For a car parts company, I worked as a mechanic after graduating.
C. After graduating, I worked as a mechanic for a car parts company.
D. I worked as a mechanic after graduating for a car parts company.

My degree in Psychology is, I believe, a distinct benefit for a sales position at your dealership. Many of the courses I took involved 5. Select... ▼ This has given me a deeper understanding of how people respond to different types of incentives and triggers so I can analyze what inspires them to buy.

5. Select... ▼
A. the study of how humans think and thinking affects behavior.
B. the study of humans thinking and how thinking affects behavior.
C. the study of how humans think and how to think affects behavior.
D. the study of how humans think and how thinking affects behavior.

I welcome 6. Select... ▼ with you in person.

6. Select... ▼
A. the opportunity to discuss my qualifications
B. the opportunity for to discuss my qualifications
C. the opportunity for discussing my qualifications
D. the opportunity of discussing my qualifications

Thank you for your consideration. I look forward to hearing from you.
Sincerely,

Darius Miller

Use the pair of passages to answer Questions 7–16.

Adapted from Senate Floor Statement on the Minimum Wage by Senator Al Franken (D), April 30, 2014

1   Now, the economy is getting better. But raising the minimum wage is about doing everything we can to make sure it gets better for everyone. Last year, our nation's largest businesses saw record profits. The stock market finished up last year up over 26 percent—its best return since the 1990s. Raising the minimum wage is about making sure that Minnesotans and workers across the country get to be a part of the improving economy.

2   That's why Minnesota has taken this important step. We know that a strong minimum wage and a strong middle class go hand in hand. That's why I support raising the federal minimum wage to a level that allows people to work their way to a better life. For decades, the federal minimum wage has lost its value. If the federal minimum wage had kept pace with inflation since its peak value in the 1960s, today it would be worth over ten dollars and fifty cents an hour. Today, the federal minimum is just seven dollars and twenty-five cents. So while families have had to pay more—for food, rent, utilities, child care, and education—the minimum wage hasn't kept up.

3   Bringing the minimum wage back to a level that can support a family is the first step in restoring the promise that if you work hard, you can build a better life for yourself and your family. Sometimes people ask why raise the wage to $9.50 or $10.10. They say, why not leave minimum wage workers alone to figure things out themselves. Now, I don't believe that raising the minimum wage is going to solve all the problems that working families face today. They need more than a minimum wage—they need good jobs, good schools, and good roads to provide a better future for themselves and their children. But I support raising the minimum wage to $10.10 because it's a wage that says America values work. It's a minimum guarantee that anyone who shows up 40 hours a week and ready to work should be able to provide food and shelter for themselves and their children and should not live in poverty.

4   Other people say that we don't need to raise the minimum wage because it's not working families who earn the minimum wage. Instead they say it's mainly teenagers in their first job who earn the minimum wage. But in fact, the vast majority of the workers who would get a raise under this bill are working adults, including approximately 350,000 adults in Minnesota. One-quarter are parents, including over 85,000 parents in our state. The parents who would see a raise from the bill we are considering are the parents of 14 million children. . . . Nationwide, one in five working mothers would see a raise under this bill. And 6.8 million workers and their families would be lifted out of poverty.

Excerpted from the Senate Republican Policy Committee position paper "Minimum Wage Increase Is Bad for Jobs." (April 1, 2014)

CBO Predicts Job Loss from Minimum Wage Increase

1. The nonpartisan Congressional Budget Office *expects* the Democrats' minimum wage plan would reduce total employment by about 500,000 workers—and by as many as one million.

CBO estimated effect of a $10.10/hour minimum wage	
	Change in employment
Central estimate	–500,000 workers
Upper end of likely range	–1,000,000 workers

2. Democrats assert that raising the minimum wage will help low-wage workers. On the contrary, a study last year found that an increase in the minimum wage could actually hinder the hiring of low-wage workers. Economists at Texas A&M University estimated the loss in job growth in each state under a minimum wage of $10 an hour. The researchers found that **more than 2.3 million new jobs would be lost nationwide**. A state-by-state breakdown showed job losses ranging from 5,100 in Alaska to 219,400 in Texas.

3. Not only would an increase in the minimum wage reduce new hiring at a time when the country desperately needs jobs, it would actually tip the balance in many states from net employment gains to net losses. In all, 32 states that are currently experiencing employment growth would face a decrease in employment if the minimum wage were increased to $10 an hour.

Who Gets Hurt the Most by Increasing the Minimum Wage?

4. New data from the Labor Department show that 58.8% of all workers in 2013 were hourly workers, but only 4.3% of them are at or below the federal minimum wage. That's down from 4.7% in 2012 and 13.4% in 1979.

5. About half of all minimum wage workers are less than 25 years old. Among employed teenagers (ages 16 to 19) paid by the hour, about 20% earned the minimum wage or less, compared with 3% of workers age 25 and over. Additionally, only 2% of full-time workers were paid the minimum wage.

6   The most recent unemployment rate for teenagers was 21.4 percent. An increase in the federal minimum wage would be particularly harmful to this group struggling to get on the employment ladder. **When employer costs are arbitrarily increased, such as with an increase in the minimum wage,** they become more likely to hire experienced workers and less likely to take a chance on young workers.

7   In 2013, 19 states had minimum wages above the federal level of $7.25 per hour. An analysis of employment in these states found a one-dollar increase in the minimum wage would result in a 1.48 percentage point increase in the unemployment rate. But a one-dollar increase correlated to a 4.67 percentage point increase in teenage unemployment rate.

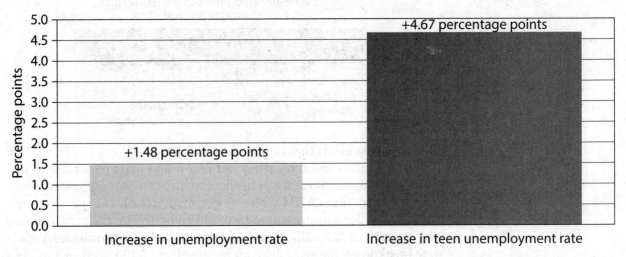

Teens bear the brunt of an increase in unemployment rate from a $1 hike in minimum wage.

7. Which is an accurate summary of paragraph 1 of Franken's speech?
    A. The economy is improving, so we do not need to increase the minimum wage.
    B. The economy is improving, and businesses have experienced record profits.
    C. The economy is improving, but minimum-wage workers do not earn enough.
    D. The economy is improving, yet workers at all levels struggle to earn enough.

8. Which is a valid reason for increasing the minimum wage, according to Franken?
    A. It would mean people were paid what they were worth.
    B. It would allow young people to save for school.
    C. It would close the gap between the rich and poor.
    D. It would help people support their families.

POSTTEST

9. In paragraph 4, how does Franken distinguish his point of view from those who disagree with his position?

    A. by posing and then answering questions they often ask
    B. by requesting that he and his opponents reach a compromise
    C. by suggesting that they care less about minimum-wage earners than he does
    D. by presenting facts and statistics to counter their arguments

10. Franken and the position paper offer different interpretations of the data about the effect of raising the minimum wage. Write one answer choice letter in each of the boxes below to identify the interpretation in each passage. (**Note**: On the actual GED® test, you will click on your choices and "drag" them into position in the chart.)

Effects of Raising the Minimum Wage	
Franken's interpretation	CBO's interpretation

    A. It will boost an ailing US economy by creating new jobs.
    B. It will give businesses a reason to hire new workers.
    C. It will raise Americans and their families out of poverty.
    D. It will result in substantial job loss and slow job growth.

11. What do Franken's speech and the position paper have in common?

    A. Both present factual evidence to support their claims.
    B. Both use an informal style to communicate their ideas.
    C. Both employ emotional appeals to sway their audiences.
    D. Both include anecdotes to illustrate their point of view.

12. The bar graph supports the CBO text's claim by showing that raising the minimum wage would

    A. help families escape poverty.
    B. raise teen unemployment.
    C. create more jobs for adults.
    D. force businesses to lose profits.

13. What conclusion can you draw from both passages?

    A. Millions of minimum-wage earners work in the United States.
    B. Most minimum-wage laborers live below the poverty line.
    C. A majority of minimum-wage workers are teenagers.
    D. More than half of working mothers hold minimum-wage jobs.

14. For each answer choice, decide if it is an implicit or an explicit reason why Franken included paragraph 4 in his speech. Then write the letter of each choice in the correct box in the chart. (**Note**: On the actual GED® test, you will click on your choices and "drag" them into position in the chart.)

Explicit Purpose	Implicit Purpose

   A. to imply that minimum-wage earners do not work hard enough
   B. to refute the claim that most minimum-wage earners are teenagers
   C. to introduce a bill for raising the minimum wage to $10.10 an hour
   D. to urge fellow senators to vote to raise the federal minimum wage

15. Paragraph 7 of the position paper builds upon paragraph 6 by

   A. illustrating the claim that millions of teens need their jobs.
   B. refuting the argument that most minimum-wage workers are teens.
   C. supporting the idea that half of minimum-wage earners are teens.
   D. supporting the point that increasing the minimum wage would hurt teens.

16. The phrase "... it's a wage that says America values work" (Franken, paragraph 4) appeals to the audience's

   A. loyalty to a political party.
   B. understanding of economics.
   C. feelings of patriotism.
   D. sense of reason.

POSTTEST

Use the passage to answer Questions 17–22.

Adapted from "What Should I Do if I See a Bear?" (US National Parks and Wildlife Website)

Avoiding an Encounter

1   Seeing a bear in the wild is a special treat for any visitor to a national park. While it is an exciting moment, it is important to remember that bears in national parks are wild and can be dangerous. Their behavior is sometimes unpredictable. Although rare, attacks on humans have occurred, inflicting serious injuries and death. Each bear and each experience is unique; there is no single strategy that will work in all situations and that guarantees safety. Most bear encounters end without injury. Following some basic guidelines may help lessen the threat of danger. Your safety can depend on your ability to calm the bear....

2   Following *viewing etiquette* is the first step to avoiding an encounter with a bear that could escalate into an attack. Keeping your distance and not surprising bears are some of the most important things you can do. Most bears will avoid humans if they hear them coming. Pay attention to your surroundings and make a special effort to be noticeable if you are in an area with known bear activity or a good food such as berry bushes.

Bear Encounters

3   Once a bear has noticed you and is paying attention to you, additional strategies can help prevent the situation from escalating.

- **Identify yourself** by talking calmly so the bear knows you are a human and not a prey animal. Remain still; stand your ground, but slowly wave your arms. Help the bear recognize you as a human. It may come closer or stand on its hind legs to get a better look or smell. A standing bear is usually curious, not threatening.

- **Stay calm** and remember that most bears do not want to attack you; they usually just want to be left alone. Bears may bluff their way out of an encounter by charging and then turning away at the last second. Bears may also react defensively by woofing, yawning, salivating, growling, snapping their jaws, and laying their ears back. Continue to talk to the bear in low tones; this will help you stay calmer, and it won't be threatening to the bear. A scream or sudden movement may trigger an attack. Never imitate bear sounds or make a high-pitched squeal.

- **Make yourselves look as large as possible** (for example, move to higher ground).

- **Do NOT allow the bear access to your food.** Getting your food will only encourage the bear and make the problem worse for others.

- **Do NOT drop your pack** as it can provide protection for your back and prevent a bear from accessing your food.

- If the bear is stationary, **move away slowly and sideways**; this allows you to keep an eye on the bear and avoid tripping. Moving sideways is also nonthreatening to bears. Do NOT run, but if the bear follows, stop and hold your ground. Bears can run as fast as a racehorse both uphill and down. Like dogs, they will chase fleeing animals. Do NOT climb a tree. Both grizzlies and black bears can climb trees. Leave the area or take a detour. If this is impossible, wait until the bear moves away. Always leave the bear an escape route.

- **Be especially cautious if you see a female with cubs**; never place yourself between a mother and her cub, and never attempt to approach them. The chances of an attack escalate greatly if she sees you as a danger to her cubs.

4 Bear attacks are rare; most bears are only interested in protecting food, cubs, or their space. However, being mentally prepared can help you have the most effective reaction. . . .

17. Using the answer choice list, identify two details from the passage that support the main idea—how to avoid a bear attack. Write one correct answer choice letter in each of the blank circles below. (**Note**: On the actual GED® test, you will click on an answer choice and "drag" it into position in the figure.)

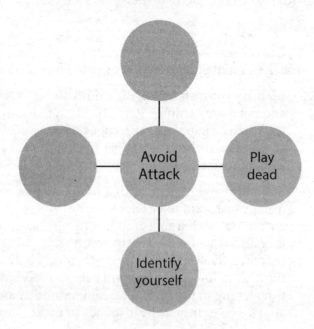

A. Talk softly.
B. Climb a tree.
C. Run away.
D. Stay calm.
E. Call for help.
F. Offer food.

18. Based on the passage, which of the following cause-and-effect relationships is accurate?

    A. Bears recognize humans and will withdraw.
    B. Bears see humans as food and will charge.
    C. Bears are curious about humans and will approach.
    D. Bears feel threatened by humans and will attack.

19. Based on the evidence, which of the following is an underlying assumption in the passage?

    A. Bears and other wildlife deserve our respect and admiration.
    B. Bears and humans share a common desire to be understood.
    C. Bears want to avoid humans as much as we want to avoid them.
    D. Bears can be unpredictable and dangerous but rarely attack.

20. Which sentence from the passage states the main idea?

    A. Bear attacks are rare; most bears are only interested in protecting food, cubs, or their space.
    B. Continue to talk to the bear in low tones; this will help you stay calmer, and it won't be threatening to the bear.
    C. Each bear and each experience is unique; there is no single strategy that will work in all situations and that guarantees safety.
    D. Be especially cautious if you see a female with cubs; never place yourself between a mother and her cub, and never attempt to approach them.

POSTTEST

Use the following excerpt to answer Question 21:

Bear attacks are rare; most bears are only interested in protecting food, cubs, or their space. However, being mentally prepared can help you have the most effective reaction.

21. How does the word *however* reinforce the author's purpose?

    A. It emphasizes the author's opinion about the rarity of bear attacks.
    B. It illustrates the author's idea that bears are only interested in food.
    C. It lets the author assure readers that a bear attack is highly unlikely.
    D. It returns to the author's point about the importance of being prepared.

22. Based on the passage, why are mother bears especially dangerous?

    A. Mother bears feel defenseless against intruders.
    B. Mother bears are extremely protective of their cubs.
    C. Mother bears perceive humans as food.
    D. Mother bears fight to protect their territory.

THIS IS THE END OF PART 1. GO ON TO PART 2.

POSTTEST
Extended Response

Part 2: 1 question | **45 minutes**

Use the following two excerpts for Item 1.

Excerpt Adapted from "The Dangers of the Proposal of the U.S. Fish and Wildlife Service to Introduce Grizzly Bears into Idaho," a Speech to the U.S. House of Representatives (July 1997) by Congresswoman Helen Chenoweth

The U.S. Fish and Wildlife Service has prepared a plan to introduce grizzly bears into a huge part of my district. Let me explain to the Members that this would affect a significant portion of the State of Idaho. The area we're talking about is over one-third of the state. Just to give Members an idea about how big this area is, let me give a comparison. In this area we could fit the states of Connecticut, Delaware, Maryland, Massachusetts, New Hampshire, Vermont, and Rhode Island, and still have over a million unfilled acres. You should be aware that the area they are talking about contains many populated regions, including the area around the University of Idaho. Moreover, the border of the grizzly bear recovery area runs very close to Boise.

The grizzly bear is a huge and dangerous animal, which makes for us a huge and dangerous problem. The grizzly bear is a large predatory mammal. And, provoked or unprovoked, it can move very quickly to viciously attack a human or an animal. In addition, the grizzly has special dietary needs. Just one of them requires between 10 and 168 square miles of land to live on, depending upon the amount of food there is in the area.

Bringing back the unpredictable grizzly bear means that people will not be able to behave or work in the way they used to in this part of Idaho. Roads normally open will have to be shut down. Hiking trails will be restricted. Camping areas will be closed. Hunting will be restricted. Livestock and logging practices will be dramatically altered. Bringing back the grizzly bear is really like allowing wildlife to take over.

It is a well-known fact that grizzly bears are often violent toward humans and animals. While settlers may have recognized the beauty of these animals, they also understood the horrible threat they pose. At the time, there was no federal act to keep them from killing these animals. Thank goodness. Lewis and Clark described in their journals the absolute terror that they and the Indians had for these animals and how difficult it was to kill a grizzly, even with several shots fired from their 18th-century guns.

When I presented to the Fish and Wildlife Service these types of concerns about human risk, they, too, recognized the danger of grizzly bears. In the past few years, because more people are vacationing in our forests and lands, attacks have increased. Even with this plan, the Fish and Wildlife Service estimates that there could be about one human injury or death each year.

Let me say for the record, Mr. Speaker, not one human death or injury resulting from a grizzly bear attack is acceptable to this Congresswoman. In fact, it should not be acceptable to anyone who values human life.

Excerpt from "Final Environmental Impact Statement (EIS) Released on Reintroduction of Grizzly Bears in the Bitterroot Ecosystem in Western Montana and Central Idaho" (2000) by the U.S. Fish and Wildlife Service

The purpose of reintroducing grizzlies would be to enhance the species' potential for recovery in the lower 48 states. An estimated 50,000 grizzly bears lived in the contiguous United States prior to European settlement. Grizzly bears have been eliminated from approximately 98 percent of their historic range in the lower 48 states. Today, approximately 1,000–1,100 grizzly bears remain in five scattered populations in Montana, Idaho, Wyoming, and Washington. Only two areas in the country (the Yellowstone ecosystem and the Northern Continental Divide ecosystem which includes Glacier National Park and the Bob Marshall Wilderness) have populations of several hundred grizzlies. The other three populations have approximately 5 to 50 grizzly bears each.

The grizzly bear is a native species of the Bitterroot ecosystem and was once common there. Grizzlies were eliminated from the Bitterroots by the 1940s after a century of intensive persecution. Of all remaining unoccupied grizzly bear habitat in the lower 48 states, the Bitterroot Mountains wilderness area has the best potential for grizzly bear recovery. This area has the components of quality grizzly bear habitat. As such, the Bitterroot ecosystem offers excellent potential to recover a healthy population of grizzly bears and to boost long-term survival and recovery prospects for this species in the contiguous United States. Recovery of endangered species, and their removal from the list of endangered species, is the ultimate goal of the Endangered Species Act.

Under the plan outlined in the EIS, the Service would reintroduce a minimum of 25 grizzly bears into 25,140 square miles of the Selway-Bitterroot Wilderness over a period of five years. The bears would be taken from areas in Canada and the United States that have healthy populations of grizzly bears living in habitats similar to those found in the Bitterroot ecosystem.

All reintroduced bears would be radio-collared and monitored to determine their movements and how they use their habitat, and to keep the public informed through media outreach of general bear locations and recovery efforts. Under the plan, the Service would only consider bears with no known history of conflicts with people for reintroduction.

POSTTEST

Suitable bears would be released at remote wilderness sites within the Bitterroot Mountains of east-central Idaho that have high-quality bear habitat and low likelihood of human encounters. By designating the reintroduced grizzly population as nonessential experimental, bears that frequent areas of high human use, act aggressively toward humans, or attack livestock would be relocated or destroyed, based on actions in the Interagency Grizzly Bear Guidelines.

1. Extended response

Analyze both texts to determine which position is best supported. Use relevant and specific evidence from both sources to support your response.

Write or type your response on a separate sheet of paper. This task may require approximately 45 minutes to complete.

THIS IS THE END OF PART 2. YOU MAY TAKE A 10-MINUTE BREAK.

POSTTEST

Part 3: 40 questions | **60 minutes**

The following letter from a purchaser of a kitchen device contains several numbered blanks, each marked "Select... ▼." Beneath each one is a set of choices. Indicate the choice from each set that is correct and belongs in the blank. (Note: On the real GED® test, the choices will appear as a "drop-down" menu. When you click on a choice, it will appear in the blank.)

Customer Service Manager
Super Mix, Inc.
2700 Melrose Way
Canton, AK 15555

Dear Mr. Sherwood:

I am a longtime customer of Super Mix products. I have purchased numerous Super Mix blending products over the years and have always been impressed with their performance and durability. However, my recent purchase [1. Select... ▼]

1. Select... ▼
A. of you're Super Juicer has left me thoroughly disappointed.
B. of your Super Juicer has left me thoroughly disappointed.
C. of your Super Juicer have left me thoroughly disappointed.
D. of your're Super Juicer have left me thoroughly disappointed.

When I first opened the Super Juicer box, I found an array of small parts [2. Select... ▼] together. The instruction manual for the assembly of the device was written in poorly translated English. I was confused as to how some of the parts were supposed to connect. [3. Select... ▼] the manual contained complicated diagrams that were no help at all. I had to go online to watch a video of someone assembling the appliance properly, which was very time-consuming.

2. Select... ▼
A. that have to be put
B. that had to be putted
C. that had to be put
D. that has to be put

3. Select... ▼
A. In addition,
B. Therefore,
C. Consequently,
D. However,

Even after I assembled [4. Select... ▼] The juicer can handle only soft fruits such as citrus and bananas, not firmer fruits and vegetables. In fact, [5. Select... ▼] sounds as if you are overloading the machine. Considering the price tag and your company's reputation, I was expecting a juicer with much more power.

4. Select... ▼
A. the juicer, which took several hours, there was additional problems.
B. the juicer which took several hours, there were additional problems.
C. the juicer which took several hours there were additional problems.
D. the juicer, which took several hours, there were additional problems.

5. Select... ▼
A. it's motor
B. its motor
C. their motor
D. they're motor

[6. Select... ▼] I bought the product, and I will keep it. However, I would like you to consider redesigning the Super Juicer to make it more user-friendly. Also, please know that if I have a similar experience in the future with your other products, I will switch to another brand.

6. Select... ▼
A. I am not writing to ask. For a refund.
B. I am not writing to ask for a refund.
C. I am not writing. To ask for a refund.
D. I not writing to ask for a refund.

Sincerely,

Warren Brinker

Use the passage to answer Questions 7–13.

Prediabetes: Am I at Risk?

1. The Centers for Disease Control and Prevention (CDC) estimates that 1 of every 3 US adults had prediabetes in 2010. That is 79 million Americans aged 20 years or older. The vast majority of people living with prediabetes do not know they have it. A person with prediabetes has a blood sugar level higher than normal, but not high enough for a diagnosis of diabetes.

2. Prediabetes is a serious health condition that increases the risk of developing type 2 diabetes, heart disease, and stroke. Seventy-nine million Americans—35% of adults aged 20 years and older—have prediabetes. Half of all Americans aged 65 years and older have prediabetes. Without lifestyle changes to improve their health, 15% to 30% of people with prediabetes will develop type 2 diabetes within 5 years.

How can type 2 diabetes be prevented?

3. Research shows that modest weight loss and regular physical activity can help prevent or delay type 2 diabetes by up to 58% in people with prediabetes. Modest weight loss means 5% to 7% of body weight, which is 10 to 14 pounds for a 200-pound person. Getting at least 150 minutes each week of physical activity, such as brisk walking, also is important.

4. The lifestyle change program offered through the National Diabetes Prevention Program—led by the CDC—can help participants adopt the healthy habits needed to prevent type 2 diabetes. Trained lifestyle coaches lead classes to help participants improve their food choices, increase physical activity, and learn coping skills to maintain weight loss and healthy lifestyle changes.

5. Many factors increase your risk for prediabetes and type 2 diabetes. To find out more about your risk, see which characteristics in this list apply to you.

- I am 45 years of age or older.
- I am overweight.
- I have a parent, sister, or brother with diabetes.
- My family background is African American, Hispanic/Latino, American Indian, Asian American, or Pacific Islander.
- I had diabetes while I was pregnant (gestational diabetes), or I gave birth to a baby weighing 9 pounds or more.
- I am physically active less than three times a week.

POSTTEST

6   It is important to find out early if you have prediabetes or type 2 diabetes, because early treatment can prevent serious problems that diabetes can cause, such as loss of eyesight or kidney damage. If you are 45 years of age or older, you should consider getting a blood test from a health care provider for prediabetes and diabetes, especially if you are overweight. . . .

7   If your blood test results indicate you have prediabetes, you should enroll in an evidence-based lifestyle change program to lower your chances of getting type 2 diabetes. Studies show that people with prediabetes can prevent or delay type 2 diabetes by losing 5% to 7% of their weight—that is 10 to 14 pounds for a 200-pound person. Weight loss should be achieved by making modest lifestyle changes to improve nutrition and increase physical activity. . . .

National Diabetes Statistics Report, 2014

Diagnosed and undiagnosed diabetes in the United States, all ages, 2012

Total: 29.1 million people or 9.3% of the population have diabetes.

Diagnosed: 21.0 million people.

Undiagnosed: 8.1 million people (27.8% of people) with diabetes are undiagnosed.

Diagnosed and undiagnosed diabetes among people aged 20 years or older, United States, 2012

	Number with diabetes (millions)	Percentage with diabetes (unadjusted)
Total		
20 years or older	28.9	12.3
By age		
20–44	4.3	4.1
45–64	13.4	16.2
65 years or older	11.2	25.9
By sex		
Men	15.5	13.6
Women	13.4	11.2

[adapted from http://www.cdc.gov/diabetes/prevention/prediabetes.htm/685]

POSTTEST

7. What main idea can you infer from reading the passage?

    A. One in three Americans has undiagnosed type 2 diabetes.
    B. People who are 45 years old should get a test for type 2 diabetes.
    C. There are several methods to diagnose if one has type 2 diabetes.
    D. Lifestyle changes can prevent or delay the development of type 2 diabetes.

8. What role do the details in the bulleted list play in this article?

    A. They outline the steps one can take to help prevent type 2 diabetes.
    B. They describe the tests available for detecting type 2 diabetes.
    C. They identify the most common risk factors for type 2 diabetes.
    D. They show the numbers of Americans who have type 2 diabetes.

9. How is the table different from the text?

    A. It targets a different audience.
    B. It covers a different aspect of the topic.
    C. It has a different purpose.
    D. It reaches a different conclusion.

10. What conclusion can you draw from reading the text and the table?

    A. Millions of Americans have been diagnosed with diabetes and prediabetes.
    B. Most Americans are overweight and have weight-related health issues.
    C. Many Americans have participated in the CDC's prevention program.
    D. A majority of Americans over 45 years of age are living with prediabetes.

Use the following excerpt to answer Question 11:

Modest weight loss means 5% to 7% of body weight, which is 10 to 14 pounds for a 200-pound person.

11. Which word could be used in place of the word *modest*?

    A. proper
    B. shy
    C. plain
    D. limited

12. How does paragraph 2 help develop the author's ideas?

    A. It outlines activities that can help prevent type 2 diabetes.
    B. It identifies segments of the American population with diabetes.
    C. It explains the relationship between prediabetes and type 2 diabetes.
    D. It provides a list of factors that increase one's risk of prediabetes.

13. People in which age group are most likely to have diabetes? Place an X on the blank next to your choice. (**Note:** On the actual GED test, you will click on the blank to place an X on it.)

    _____ 20–44
    _____ 45–64
    _____ 65+

Excerpt from *My Antonia* by Willa Cather

1. When grandmother was ready to go, I said I would like to stay up there in the garden awhile.

2. She peered down at me from under her sunbonnet. 'Aren't you afraid of snakes?'

3. 'A little,' I admitted, 'but I'd like to stay, anyhow.'

4. 'Well, if you see one, don't have anything to do with him. The big yellow and brown ones won't hurt you; they're bull snakes and help to keep the gophers down. Don't be scared if you see anything look out of that hole in the bank over there. That's a badger hole. He's about as big as a big 'possum, and his face is striped, black and white. He takes a chicken once in a while, but I won't let the men harm him. In a new country a body feels friendly to the animals. I like to have him come out and watch me when I'm at work.'

5. Grandmother swung the bag of potatoes over her shoulder and went down the path, leaning forward a little. The road followed the windings of the draw; when she came to the first bend, she waved at me and disappeared. I was left alone with this new feeling of lightness and content.

6. I sat down in the middle of the garden, where snakes could scarcely approach unseen, and leaned my back against a warm yellow pumpkin. There were some ground-cherry bushes growing along the furrows, full of fruit. I turned back the papery triangular sheaths that protected the berries and ate a few. All about me giant grasshoppers, twice as big as any I had ever seen, were doing acrobatic feats among the dried vines. The gophers scurried up and down the ploughed ground. There in the sheltered draw-bottom the wind did not blow very hard, but I could hear it singing its humming tune up on the level, and I could see the tall grasses wave. The earth was warm under me, and warm as I crumbled it through my fingers. Queer little red bugs came out and moved in slow squadrons around me. Their backs were polished vermilion, with black spots. I kept as still as I could. Nothing happened. I did not expect anything to happen. I was something that lay under the sun and felt it, like the pumpkins, and I did not want to be anything more. I was entirely happy. Perhaps we feel like that when we die and become a part of something entire, whether it is sun and air, or goodness and knowledge. At any rate, that is happiness; to be dissolved into something complete and great. When it comes to one, it comes as naturally as sleep.

14. Based on details in the passage, choose two words from the answer choices that describe how the setting makes the narrator feel. Write the letters of your choices in the blank circles below. (**Note**: On the actual GED® test, you will click on your choices and "drag" them into position.)

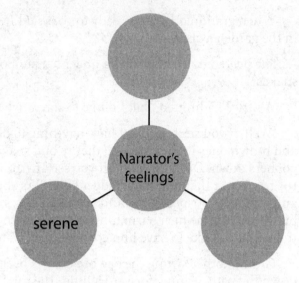

A. comforted
B. relieved
C. nostalgic
D. blissful

15. Which of the following *best* states a theme of the story?

A. Facing one's fears is important in life.
B. Sitting quietly alone leads to great insights.
C. Spending time with animals is life changing.
D. Connecting with nature can lead to deep happiness.

Use the following excerpt to answer Questions 16 and 17:

I was left alone with this new feeling of lightness and content.

16. Which word would change the meaning of the sentence if it replaced *content*?

    A. harmony
    B. tranquility
    C. satisfaction
    D. drowsiness

17. Reread the excerpt. Based on it, what can you infer about the narrator?

    A. He is experiencing deep loneliness.
    B. He is relieved to be by himself.
    C. He is enjoying unexpected emotions.
    D. He is waiting for something to happen.

18. How do the narrator and the grandmother feel about wild animals? Overall,

    A. she is fearful; he is attentive.
    B. she is accepting; he is nervous.
    C. she is indifferent; he is curious.
    D. she is friendly; he is unimpressed.

19. Which of the following events happens last in the story?

    A. The narrator considers the nature of life and death.
    B. The narrator wonders at his newfound happiness.
    C. The narrator marvels at the insect life in the garden.
    D. The narrator realizes how much he loves his family.

20. Place an X on the blank next to each item that the narrator sees in the garden. (**Note:** On the actual GED test, you will click on the blank to place an X on it.)

    _____ pumpkins
    _____ strawberries
    _____ ground cherries
    _____ a snake
    _____ a badger
    _____ gophers
    _____ grasshoppers

Use the passage below to answer questions 21–27.

President Eisenhower's Special Message to the Congress Regarding a National Highway Program, February 22, 1955

1   Our unity as a nation is sustained by free communication of thought and by easy transportation of people and goods. The ceaseless flow of information throughout the Republic is matched by individual and commercial movement over a vast system of interconnected highways criss-crossing the country and joining at our national borders with friendly neighbors to the north and south.

2   Together, the uniting forces of our communication and transportation systems are dynamic elements in the very name we bear—United States. Without them, we would be a mere alliance of many separate parts.

3   The Nation's highway system is a gigantic enterprise, one of our largest items of capital investment. Generations have gone into its building. Three million, three hundred and sixty-six thousand miles of road, travelled by 58 million motor vehicles, comprise it. The replacement cost of its drainage and bridge and tunnel works is incalculable. One in every seven Americans gains his livelihood and supports his family out of it. But, in large part, the network is inadequate for the nation's growing needs.

4   First: Each year, more than 36 thousand people are killed and more than a million injured on the highways. To the home where the tragic aftermath of an accident on an unsafe road is a gap in the family circle, the monetary worth of preventing that death cannot be reckoned. But reliable estimates place the measurable economic cost of the highway accident toll to the Nation at more than $4.3 billion a year.

5   Second: The physical condition of the present road net increases the cost of vehicle operation, according to many estimates, by as much as one cent per mile of vehicle travel. At the present rate of travel, this totals more than $5 billion a year. The cost is not borne by the individual vehicle operator alone. It pyramids into higher expense of doing the nation's business. Increased highway transportation costs, passed on through each step in the distribution of goods, are paid ultimately by the individual consumer.

6   Third: In case of an atomic attack on our key cities, the road net must permit quick evacuation of target areas, mobilization of defense forces and maintenance of every essential economic function. But the present system in critical areas would be the breeder of a deadly congestion within hours of an attack.

POSTTEST

7   Fourth: Our Gross National Product, about $357 billion in 1954, is estimated to reach over $500 billion in 1965 when our population will exceed 180 million and, according to other estimates, will travel in 81 million vehicles 814 billion vehicle miles that year. Unless the present rate of highway improvement and development is increased, existing traffic jams only faintly foreshadow those of ten years hence.

8   To correct these deficiencies is an obligation of Government at every level. The highway system is a public enterprise. As the owner and operator, the various levels of Government have a responsibility for management that promotes the economy of the nation and properly serves the individual user. In the case of the Federal Government, moreover, expenditures on a highway program are a return to the highway user of the taxes which he pays in connection with his use of the highways. . . .

21. Which sentence from the passage supports President Eisenhower's claim that the nation's highway system was "a gigantic enterprise"?

    A. Together, the uniting forces of our communication and transportation systems are dynamic elements in the very name we bear—United States.
    B. Three million, three hundred and sixty-six thousand miles of road, travelled by 58 million motor vehicles, comprise it.
    C. Our Gross National Product, about $357 billion in 1954, is estimated to reach over $500 billion in 1965 when our population will exceed 180 million.
    D. In the case of the Federal Government, moreover, expenditures on a highway program are a return to the highway user of the taxes which he pays.

22. Which statement supports Eisenhower's claim that the highway system needed safety improvements?

    A. The cost of vehicle operation was more than five billion dollars.
    B. The highway system served 65 percent of urban traffic.
    C. Fifty-eight million vehicles travelled the nation's highways.
    D. Thirty-six thousand people died or were injured on highways.

23. In paragraphs 4–7, President Eisenhower advances the claim that the American highway system is inadequate by

    A. restating his claim about highways uniting the nation.
    B. connecting highways to American national pride.
    C. sharing motorists' complaints about driving the highways.
    D. listing the consequences of failing to invest in highways.

24. How does paragraph 8 further develop paragraphs 4–7?

    A. It explains the effects of the actions described in paragraphs 4–7.
    B. It outlines a solution for the problems noted in paragraphs 4–7.
    C. It describes the highway system referred to in paragraphs 4–7.
    D. It provides examples to support the claims in paragraphs 4–7.

25. What is President Eisenhower's purpose for giving this speech?

    A. to explain why an expanded highway system is necessary
    B. to argue that greater safety is needed in the highway system
    C. to convince Americans to invest in a new federal highway system
    D. to define the difference between federal and state highway systems

26. Which claim made by Eisenhower lacks relevant supporting evidence?

    A. The highway system is inadequate for a growing nation.
    B. Improved highways promise a good return on drivers' tax dollars.
    C. Highway accidents cost the nation more than four billion dollars a year.
    D. The interstate highway system connects only forty-two states.

27. In paragraph 4, what does Eisenhower mean by "a gap in the family circle"?

    A. a missing relative
    B. a single-parent home
    C. an accidental death
    D. lost income

Use the passage to answer Questions 28–34.

Adapted from *Heidi* by Johanna Spyri (Translated by Elisabeth P. Stork)

1   One bright sunny morning in June, a tall, vigorous maiden of the mountain region climbed up the narrow path, leading a little girl by the hand. The youngster's cheeks were in such a glow that it showed even through her sun-browned skin. Small wonder though! For in spite of the heat, the little one, who was scarcely five years old, was bundled up as if she had to brave a bitter frost. Her shape was difficult to distinguish, for she wore two dresses, if not three, and around her shoulders a large red cotton shawl. With her feet encased in heavy hob-nailed boots, this hot and shapeless little person toiled up the mountain.

2   The pair had been climbing for about an hour when they reached a hamlet[1] halfway up the great mountain named the Alm. This hamlet was called "Im Dörfli" or "The Little Village." It was the elder girl's home town, and therefore she was greeted from nearly every house . . . ; a voice called out to her through an open door: "Deta, please wait one moment! I am coming with you, if you are going further up."

3   When the girl stood still to wait, the child instantly let go her hand and promptly sat down on the ground.

4   "Are you tired, Heidi?" Deta asked the child.

5   "No, but hot," she replied.

6   "We shall be up in an hour, if you take big steps and climb with all your little might!" Thus the elder girl tried to encourage her small companion.

7   A stout, pleasant-looking woman stepped out of the house and joined the two. The child had risen and wandered behind the old acquaintances, who immediately started gossiping about their friends in the neighborhood and the people of the hamlet generally.

8   "Where are you taking the child, Deta?" asked the newcomer. "Is she the child your sister left?"

9   "Yes," Deta assured her; "I am taking her up to the Alm-Uncle and there I want her to remain."

10   "You can't really mean to take her there Deta. You must have lost your senses, to go to him. I am sure the old man will show you the door and won't even listen to what you say."

---

[1] hamlet: small village

11   "Why not? As he's her grandfather, it is high time he should do something for the child. I have taken care of her until this summer and now a good place has been offered to me. The child shall not hinder me from accepting it, I tell you that!"

12   "It would not be so hard, if he were like other mortals. But you know him yourself. How could he *look* after a child, especially such a little one? She'll never get along with him, I am sure of that!—But tell me of your prospects."

13   "I am going to a splendid house in Frankfurt. Last summer some people went off to the baths and I took care of their rooms. As they got to like me, they wanted to take me along, but I could not leave. They have come back now and have persuaded me to go with them."

14   "I am glad I am not the child!" exclaimed Barbara with a shudder. "Nobody knows anything about the old man's life up there. He doesn't speak to a living soul, and from one year's end to the other he keeps away from church. People get out of his way when he appears once in a twelve-month down here among us. We all fear him . . . with those thick grey eyebrows and that huge uncanny beard. When he wanders along the road with his twisted stick we are all afraid to meet him alone."

15   "That is not my fault," said Deta stubbornly. "He won't do her any harm; and if he should, he is responsible, not I."

28. How does the structure of paragraph 1 support the author's purpose?

    A. It foreshadows an important aspect of the story's theme.
    B. It describes the setting and the characters in the story.
    C. It introduces the conflict between the story's characters.
    D. It illustrates the most intense moment in the story.

29. Place the events of the story in the correct order by writing each answer choice letter in the appropriate box. (**Note**: On the actual GED® test, you will click on each choice and "drag" it into position in the chart.)

1.
2.
3.
4.

    A. Deta listens to Barbara question her decision to take Heidi up the mountain.
    B. Deta does not pause for any conversation as villagers call out to her.
    C. Deta holds Heidi's hand as they walk up the steep mountain trail.
    D. Deta explains that she has been offered a good job and plans to take it.

POSTTEST

30. According to the village woman, what is Heidi's grandfather like?

    A. He has a secret wish to see his granddaughter Heidi.
    B. He has a reputation in the village as a gossip.
    C. He has a dark past that no one will talk about.
    D. He has a gruff manner and spends his time alone.

31. What is the conflict in the story?

    A. Heidi does not want to go live with her grandfather.
    B. The villagers do not want Heidi to live among them.
    C. Deta does not want to care for Heidi but rather to take a job.
    D. The village woman does not want to hear Deta's gossip.

32. What is the relationship between Deta and Barbara?

    A. They are friends.
    B. Barbara is Deta's sister.
    C. They are neighbors.
    D. Deta is Barbara's niece.

33. Which word has the same connotation as *toiled*, as it is used in paragraph 1?

    A. strolled
    B. worked
    C. trudged
    D. sprang

34. Deta is Heidi's _____. Fill in the blank with the correct relationship. (**Note:** On the actual GED test, you will click on the blank and then type your response.)

The following letter contains several numbered blanks, each marked "Select...." Beneath each one is a set of choices. Indicate the choice from each set that is correct and belongs in the blank. (Note: On the real GED test, the choices will appear as a "drop-down" menu. When you click on a choice, it will appear in the blank.)

Diggers Hotline,

April is [35. Select...▼] With the approach of spring, the snow begins to disappear. Homeowners want to get started on outdoor projects and [36. Select...▼] It's understandable.

35. Select... ▼
A. national safe digging month.
B. National Safe Digging Month.
C. National safe digging month.
D. national Safe Digging month.

36. Select... ▼
A. are hoping to get them done quickly.
B. are hoping to get it done quickly.
C. hope to get it done quickly.
D. hope to get them done quickly.

Before starting on any project that requires digging, all homeowners and contractors must call the Diggers Hotline at the toll-free number: (800) DIGGERS. According to state law, anyone digging must call the hotline at least three business days before starting work. The caller must provide information on [37. Select...▼] Diggers Hotline contacts the local utility company. The utility company then [38. Select...▼] They mark the underground cables or pipes with spray paint and colored flags. After that, the digging can proceed safely.

37. Select... ▼
A. the type of work, the location, and the type of equipment to be used.
B. the type of work the location and the type of equipment to be used.
C. the type of work, the location and the type of equipment to be used.
D. the type of work; the location, and the type of equipment to be used.

38. Select...
A.	sent out technicians.
B.	sends out technicians.
C.	send out technicians.
D.	sending out technicians.

Diggers Hotline helps avoid damaging homes. Nationally, [39. Select...] that occur when excavating work is performed. [40. Select...] it is important to call before you dig.

39. Select...
A.	every year their are more than 200,000 accidents
B.	every year they're are more than 200,000 accidents
C.	every year there are more than 200,000 accidents
D.	every year there are more then 200,000 accidents

40. Select...
A.	These could be prevented but that's why
B.	These could be prevented, but that's why
C.	These could be prevented and that's why
D.	These could be prevented, and that's why

THIS IS THE END OF THE REASONING THROUGH LANGUAGE ARTS (RLA) POSTTEST. ANSWERS AND EXPLANATIONS BEGIN ON THE NEXT PAGE.

Answers and Explanations

Part 1

1. Choice **C** correctly uses capitalization and does not include any unnecessary commas.
2. Choice **B** is correct. It is the only choice that is not a run-on or fragment.
3. Choice **A** is correct. The word *cousins* should not be possessive. The pronoun *their* is correct.
4. Choice **C** is correct. It is the only choice that places the modifying phrases in a logical order.
5. Choice **D** is correct. It is the only choice that is balanced and parallel.
6. Choice **A** is correct. The correct idiomatic expression is *opportunity to*.
7. Choice **C** is correct. It covers all the main points in the correct order.
8. Choice **D** is correct. He supports raising the minimum wage so that people can "support a family."
9. Choice **D** is correct. Franken provides statistics to show that the opposition is incorrect.
10. Choice **C** is correct for Franken's interpretation. He says that raising the minimum wage will help people escape poverty. Choice **D** is correct for the position paper's interpretation. It says a raise in the minimum wage will slow job growth.
11. Choice **A** is correct. Both documents support their claims with facts and statistics.
12. Choice **B** is correct. The bar graph explicitly shows how a raise in the minimum wage will cause the unemployment of teens to skyrocket.
13. Choice **A** is correct. It is the answer that can be concluded from reading both texts.
14. Choice **B** is Franken's explicit, or stated, purpose—to refute a claim about minimum wage earners. Choice **D** is the implicit, or unstated, purpose—to get fellow senators to support a hike in the minimum wage.
15. Choice **D** is correct. The position paper cites experts and studies to support its argument that an increased minimum wage will increase teen unemployment.
16. Choice **C** is correct. The phrase appeals to the audience's emotions about patriotism.
17. Choices **A** and **D** are correct. Talking softly and staying calm are two ways to avoid a bear attack, according to the passage.
18. Choice **A** is correct. Bears generally leave humans alone.
19. Choice **C** is correct. The authors assume that bears and humans want to avoid each other as much as possible.
20. Choice **C** is correct. The main idea is that every bear is different, so it is important to be prepared for many different situations.
21. Choice **D** is correct. The word *however* takes readers back to the author's main point about being prepared in case of a bear attack.
22. Choice **B** is correct. Mother bears are dangerous because they are protective of their cubs.

Part 2

If possible, ask an instructor to evaluate your essay. Your instructor's opinions and comments will help you determine what skills you need to practice to improve your writing skills. You may also want to evaluate your essay yourself, using the checklist that follows. The more items you can check, the more confident you can be about your writing skills. Items that are not checked will show you the essay-writing skills that you need to work on.

POSTTEST

My essay

- creates a sound, logical argument based on the passage.
- cites evidence from the passage to support the argument.
- analyzes the issue and/or evaluates the validity of the arguments in the passage.
- organizes ideas in a sensible sequence.
- shows clear connections between main ideas.
- uses largely correct sentence structure.
- follows Standard English conventions in regard to grammar, spelling, and punctuation.

Part 3

1. Choice **B** is correct. It correctly uses the singular verb *has* and the pronoun *your*.
2. Choice **C** correctly uses the past tense *had to be put* to agree with *found*.
3. Choice **A** is correct. It is the only choice that uses a logical transitional word.
4. Choice **D** is correct. It correctly uses commas and the plural verb *were*.
5. Choice **B** is correct. The possessive pronoun *its* refers to the juicer.
6. Choice **B** is correct. It is the only complete sentence.
7. Choice **D** is correct. The main idea is that many Americans have prediabetes, but if they make lifestyle changes, they can reduce their risk of developing type 2 diabetes.
8. Choice **C** is correct. The list includes risk factors for prediabetes.
9. Choice **B** is correct. The table focuses on Americans with diabetes, not prediabetes.
10. Choice **A** is correct. The text addresses the millions of Americans living with prediabetes; the table addresses the millions of Americans diagnosed with diabetes.
11. Choice **D** is correct. Based on the context, *limited* is the best synonym for *modest*.
12. Choice **C** is correct. Paragraph 2 explains the relationship between prediabetes and type 2 diabetes.
13. 65+ is correct because that group has the highest percentage of diabetes, 25.9%. The age group 45–64 has more people with diabetes, but a much lower percentage because it is a more populous group.
14. Choices **A** and **D** are correct. Lying in the sunshine in the garden makes the narrator feel comforted and blissful.
15. Choice **D** is correct. The narrator experiences deep happiness while lying in the garden.
16. Choice **D** is correct. The word *drowsiness* would suggest a lack of awareness.
17. Choice **C** is correct. The narrator experiences "new lightness and content."
18. Choice **B** is correct. The grandmother is mostly accepting; the narrator is "a little" afraid.
19. Choice **A** is correct. The last thing to happen in the story is that the narrator considers what death might be like: "to be dissolved into something complete and great."
20. In paragraph 6, the narrator sees **pumpkins**, **gophers**, **grasshoppers**, and **ground cherries**. Snakes and badgers are talked about in paragraph 4 but are not actually seen.
21. Choice **B** is correct. These statistics indicate the highway system is huge.
22. Choice **D** is correct. It is the only piece of evidence related to highway safety.
23. Choice **D** is correct. President Eisenhower enumerates four important points about the inadequacy of the US federal highway system.
24. Choice **B** is correct. Eisenhower offers a solution to the problems outlined in the previous paragraphs.

25. Choice **A** is correct. Eisenhower's purpose is to persuade listeners by explaining why an expanded highway system is necessary.

26. Choice **B** is correct. Although it is a possible outcome of Eisenhower's plan, his claim is not supported by factual evidence.

27. Choice **C** is correct. Paragraph 4 is about traffic accidents and he talks about "preventing that death."

28. Choice **B** is correct. The paragraph is descriptive. Its purpose is to establish the setting and characters.

29. The order of events is **C, B, A, D**.

30. Choice **D** is correct. The story details suggest that the grandfather is a loner whose gruff manner inspires fear.

31. Choice **C** is correct. Deta is taking Heidi to her grandfather because she wants to take a job, not care for her orphaned niece.

32. Choice **A** is correct. Deta and Barbara are "old acquaintances."

33. Choice **C** is correct. The word *trudged* has the same negative connotation as *toiled*.

34. Deta is Heidi's **aunt**. In paragraph 8, Barbara asks Deta if Heidi is her sister's child.

35. Choice **B** correctly capitalizes every word of the title.

36. Choice **D** uses parallel construction between the simple present tense verb *want* and the verb *hope*.

37. Choice **A** correctly separates every item in the list with a comma.

38. Choice **B** correctly uses the present tense verb *sends*.

39. Choice **C** uses the correct homonym of *there* and the correct comparison word *than*.

40. **D** It correctly uses a comma to separate the independent clauses and uses the conjunction *and* to show similar ideas.

POSTTEST

Evaluation Chart

Circle the item number of each item you missed. In the left column, you will find the names of the chapters that cover the skills you need to improve. More numbers circled in any row means more attention is needed to sharpen those skills for the GED Test.

Chapter	Part 1 Questions	Part 3 Questions
Chapter 1: Grammar and Conventions	1, 2, 3, 4, 5, 6	1, 2, 3, 4, 5, 6, 35, 36, 37, 38, 39, 40
Chapter 2: Informational Texts	17, 18, 19, 20, 21, 22	7, 8, 9, 10, 11, 12, 13
Chapter 3: Argumentation and Persuasion	7, 8, 9, 10, 11, 12, 13, 14, 15, 16	21, 22, 23, 24, 25, 26, 27
Chapter 4: Literature	n/a	14, 15, 16, 17, 18, 19, 20, 28, 29, 30, 31, 32, 33, 34

If you find you need instruction or more practice before you are ready to take the GED test, remember that we offer several excellent options:

McGraw-Hill Education Preparation for the GED Test: This book contains a complete test preparation program with intensive review and practice for the topics tested on the GED.

McGraw-Hill Education Pre-GED: This book is a beginner's guide for students who need to develop a solid foundation or refresh basic skills before they embark on formal preparation for the GED test.

McGraw-Hill Education Short Course for the GED: This book provides a concise review of all the essential topics on the GED, with numerous additional practice questions.